# In Our Own Voices

*A Guide to
Conducting
Life History
Interviews
with American
Jewish Women*

◇◇◇◇◇◇◇◇◇◇◇◇◇◇◇◇◇

JAYNE K. GUBERMAN, Editor

Photographs by Joan Roth
Introduction by Joyce Antler

Jewish
Women's
Archive

*jwa. org*
where history
lives and grows

# In Our Own Voices
A Guide to Conducting Life History Interviews
with American Jewish Women
◇◇◇◇◇◇◇◇◇◇◇◇◇◇◇◇◇◇◇◇◇◇◇◇◇◇◇◇

Jewish Women's Archive
138 Harvard Street
Brookline, MA 02446
Tel: 617/232-2258
www.jwa.org
webmaster@jwa.org

GAIL T. REIMER, Executive Director
NICKI NEWMAN TANNER, Chair, Board of Directors
BARBARA DOBKIN, Founding Chair, Board of Directors

This guide is made possible through the generous
support of Muriel Hurovitz, with additional support
from the Alex Shulman Family Foundation,
the Brenda Brown Lipitz Rever Foundation,
and Mildred Guberman Kravetz.

Designer: Rena Anderson Sokolow
Text Editor: Alison Kahn

*The mission of the Jewish Women's Archive (JWA)
is to uncover, chronicle, and transmit the rich history
of American Jewish women and their contributions
to our families and our communities, to our people
and our world.*

# 'Without roots we cannot grow.

Nina Lederkremer

# CONTENTS

# PREFACE

BY Nicki Newman Tanner

*Chair, Jewish Women's Archive Board of Directors*

THE JEWISH WOMEN'S ARCHIVE TAKES GREAT PRIDE IN PRESENTING our first Oral History Guide. This guide is for everyone — teachers and students, mothers and daughters, fathers and sons, historians and community members, scholars and activists. We extend a special welcome to all oral historians, present and future.

I have been an oral historian for over twenty-five years, and I can't think of a better method for capturing and preserving what it means to grow up Jewish and female in twentieth-century America — providing critical material for the historic record.

## ORAL HISTORY HAS SEVERAL ADVANTAGES OVER OTHER HISTORICAL SOURCES:

◆ It serves as an antidote to the digital age. Historians and scholars of an earlier time could rely on correspondence and diaries. Today these forms of communication are anachronisms in an instant-message world of cell phones and email.

◆ It provides information of a different kind. Yes, we can read newspaper articles, speeches, magazine profiles, or minutes of meetings. But the personal and private experiences, the hopes, aspirations, disappointments — in short, the "meat on the bones" of the story — are rarely revealed through those reports and records.

◆ It helps us to learn about the perspective of those who do not appear in the historical record. Women's contributions have been missing from the account of the American Jewish experience.

The members of the Jewish Women's Archive believe that our voices need to become part of the larger story. Women's stories — yours, and those of your mother, grandmothers, and other significant women in your life — matter.

◆ It allows us to ask the questions that are important to us. Suppose we were studying Emma Lazarus and had a burning question about her life. Usually we can only hope that we might find an answer to our question through a creative reading of existing sources. As oral historians, however, we can ask what we want to ask and create source materials that reflect what we value and miss in conventional accounts of women's lives.

With the help of this guide, you will become a partner in JWA's mission "to uncover, chronicle, and transmit the rich legacy of Jewish women." As an oral historian, you will learn how to reach beyond facts and encourage your heroines to reflect on their lives.

The rewards will be many. With every first-hand account gathered, we learn more about the significant contributions that American Jewish women have made and are making in their communities, across the nation, and around the world. In turn, through their stories, these women will serve as new role models and new "shoulders to stand on" for those of us who follow in their footsteps, working to make the world a better place. And finally, because the oral history interview offers a rich opportunity for human interaction and friendship, you will have a wonderful time in the process.

# FOREWORD

BY Jayne K. Guberman

*Director of Oral History, Jewish Women's Archive*

JEWISH WOMEN HAVE ALWAYS BEEN TELLERS OF STORIES. ACROSS THE family table, by a child's bedside, in the kitchen, and in countless other intimate situations, generations of women have used stories to transmit family history, impart values, and foster community. Most of these stories have been ephemeral, belonging mainly to the moment of their telling. Only in recent decades have new technologies and ways of thinking about history encouraged us to capture women's voices on tape and video. Family members, scholars, and community institutions all have recorded interviews with influential women. Yet few of these interviews have focused on the women themselves and their impact on the changing world around them. Even today, women's voices remain conspicuously absent from our history books and their contributions are still relegated to the margins of our collective story.

Since its founding in 1995, the Jewish Women's Archive has engaged Jewish women across America as "makers of history." Inspired by the urgent need to collect the stories of our matriarchs, women whose lives spanned the twentieth century, JWA pioneered the use of community-based oral history projects in Boston, Seattle, and Baltimore. Working with volunteers and trained oral historians, JWA's *Weaving Women's Words* and *Women Whose Lives Span the Century* oral history projects set out to capture the life histories of a pivotal generation of women whose experiences reflect the diversity of Jewish women's lives and the impact on their families, their communities, and the world.

*In Our Own Voices*, JWA's guide to conducting life histories with American Jewish women, makes available to you the broad experience that we have garnered over years of doing oral history work. In this guide you will learn the basic steps to preparing for and conducting an oral history interview with the important Jewish women in your

**Ruth Frankel and her sister with their parents' tea set**

own life. You will also learn what to do with the interview after the tape recorder or video camera is switched off. And, most importantly, we will offer you numerous resources on American Jewish women's history and the essential *questions to ask* in order to conduct a richly textured interview.

Over the past seven years, many people have supported JWA's oral history projects to ensure that women's voices become a part of our collective story. In particular, we are grateful to Muriel Hurovitz and to the Alex Shulman Family Foundation, the Brenda Brown Lipitz Rever Foundation, and Mildred Guberman Kravetz, whose encouragement and generosity have enabled us to produce this guide.

Many others have helped us "make history" by working on JWA's oral history projects in a variety of capacities. In particular, we wish to thank Fran Putnoi, Barbara Levy and Susan Porter, and the documentors and members of the exhibition committee at Temple Israel, Boston whose dedicated work resulted in JWA's pilot oral history project, *Women Whose Lives Span the Century.*

Over the past five years, JWA's *Weaving Women's Words* projects in Seattle and Baltimore have been made possible through a collaborative effort with women in each of these communities. We are grateful to the chairs of our community advisory boards and exhibition committees, Robin Boehler in Seattle and Brenda Brown Rever, Ros Mazur and Louise Goodman in Baltimore, as well as the dedicated work of the members of their committees. Hilary Bernstein, Leslie Straka and Shelly Hettleman served as JWA community coordinators, nurturing a complex process of community involvement in selecting the narrators and bringing the projects to fruition. Ellen Smith and Jill Vexler, the curators of JWA's exhibitions in these communities, mined thousands of pages of interview transcripts to create an inspirational portrait of a pivotal generation of American Jewish women.

For their dedicated work and on-going insights into the art of conducting women's oral history, we are grateful to our oral historians, Roz Bornstein, Elaine Eff, Marcie Cohen Ferris, Jean Freedman, and Pamela Brown Lavitt.

Portraits of the narrators in this guide are by photographer Joan Roth. For over three decades, Roth has traveled the world to photograph Jewish women in their own environments. JWA is grateful to her for her dedicated participation in *Weaving Women's Words* in Baltimore and Seattle. Her work provides a richly nuanced portrait of Jewish women in these communities and an invaluable record of American Jewish women at the turn of the twenty-first century.

We are thankful to the scholars on JWA's Academic Advisory Council who have given so generously of their expertise and knowledge. Their essays in this guide provide the historical context for thinking about the complexity of Jewish women's lives and their contributions to their families, their communities, and to the larger society. In particular, we want to thank Joyce Antler, whose commitment to gathering women's stories has nurtured JWA's oral history work from the outset and whose generous spirit has been a mainstay of this guide from the beginning.

Publication of this guide would not have been possible without the help and encouragement of key individuals who have nurtured this project at every stage. In particular, we would like to thank Meredith Kormes and Ruth Pearlstein, whose attention to detail has kept us on track. Susan Berk and Jeane Ungerleider were instrumental in helping us think through the guide's format, and Sandy Warshaw of SAGE provided feedback on issues of inclusivity. Shelly Hettlman has been an invaluable ally and contributor at every point. Alison Kahn has served as both editor and sounding board, and Rena Anderson Sokolow has brought her fine eye to the design of this guide.

Finally, we thank our narrators, the women in Boston, Baltimore and Seattle who have graciously shared their life stories with us through oral history interviews. Their candor, thoughtfulness, and willingness to share their life experiences during the interview process enriched our appreciation of the inspirational power of women's words.

"Everyone has a story," the renowned anthropologist Barbara Myerhoff taught us, and these stories "told to oneself and others can transform the world." We invite you to join with us in this important work of transforming the story we tell to future generations, a story that will include us all.

Top: Naomi Kellman, Rosalie Silber Abrams
Bottom: Micky Loveman, Minna Shavitz

# INTRODUCTION

BY Joyce Antler

*Chair, Jewish Women's Archive Academic Advisory Council*

IN HER BOOK, *The Creation of Patriarchy*, HISTORIAN GERDA LERNER, THE grand "mother of women's history," distinguishes between history as the unrecorded past — all the events of the past as recollected by human beings—and history-making, a historical creation usually left, until recent times, to a professional class of male historians. While women have always been actors and agents in history, they have been left out of most of the annals of recorded History. Yet they have not only participated in sharing the world and its work with men, they have had unique experiences and have developed their own oral traditions by which these experiences were preserved. Women's scarce presence in the written record deprives all people of a fully rendered chronicle of past events and the opportunity to draw meanings from them. When one-half of the human population is excluded from history-making, history fails to serve as a source of both collective memory and personal identity.

Because women's experiences have gone unrecorded and unrecognized, most narratives of American Jewish history offer only a partial account of our past. Marginalized or ignored, or absorbed into universalized categories of "Jews" or of "Americans," Jewish women are not represented in the diverse roles they have played or as interpreters of events they have shaped. Only by enabling Jewish women to serve as witnesses to their own experience can we restore the full panorama of their lives — as wives, mothers, grandmothers, wage-earners, immigrants, community builders, organizational heads, political activists, intellectual innovators, and religious leaders — and create a more complete, balanced, and vital historical record.

Oral history provides a wonderful tool for capturing the diverse stories of Jewish women and preserving the unique voices and living memories of individuals whose histories had previously been forgotten. The testimony provided in oral histories adds new categories of historical significance by revealing the multifaceted dimensions of women's lives as they change over time. By placing an individual in the context of her family, her community, her workplace, and the political and historical framework of her time, oral histories can greatly expand the range of data that form the stuff of history and the frameworks that order its meanings.

Every oral history is unique. The narrator tells her story in her own terms, concentrating on those aspects of her life history that are the most important to her. The subjective, personal meanings of lived experience deepen historical knowledge, providing insights into how individuals interact with the historical forces that shape their lives. As the individual tells her story, she simultaneously reinterprets as well as remembers the past; through the process of oral history, she truly becomes an historian, helping to articulate and frame the memories that bear significance.

The Jewish Women's Archive's oral history guide, *In Our Own Voices*, moves women's experiences to the center of the historical process. Capturing the individuality and fullness of women's complex roles, it highlights a set of topics that form the distinctive arenas of women's lives. The ten frameworks of the Guide – Family, Education, Work, Community Service, Jewish Identities, Home and Place, Leisure and Culture, Health and Sexuality, Women's Identities, History and World Events – suggest the multiple worlds in which women lived, both public and private, as they traversed the life course. Together the frameworks provide an inclusive umbrella for collecting stories about the past that have particular, gender-specific relevance of a kind that is unusual even for the practice of oral history.

The Guide acknowledges, for example, that women's most significant relationships often take place within their families of origin and the families that they create. Families provide expectations, values and models which give shape to women's lives, yet family relationships and the complex roles of women within families also engender tensions and conflict. In similar fashion, the Guide emphasizes the many-sided considerations that have impacted women's participation in the world of work – both inside and outside the home – as they pioneered in the workplace but also suffered from the invisibility of their contributions, the painful experiences of occupational discrimination or anti-Semitism, and the continuing struggles of balancing family life with career. It probes women's participation in the world of education, inside and outside of schools and continuously through the life course, and in the many settings in which education occurs – for example, elementary and secondary schools, colleges, universities, professional schools, Jewish supplementary and day schools, private lessons, women's clubs, associations, study groups, and education-oriented travel. Voluntarism is also explored, in connection with civic or community-based groups, both in the Jewish community and the larger society, as are Jewish women's leisure and cultural pursuits which in like fashion helped define women's identities and reflected their connections to the Jewish community and the larger society.

The Guide provides sample questions and brief descriptive essays about other vital areas of women's lives: transformations in the ways in which women have experienced illness and maintained health; changes in sexuality and marriage patterns; developments in both the public and private aspects of religious life – the home and the synagogue. It asks narrators to think about experiences of migration and settlement, their connections to region, community, and neighborhood; the place of their homes in their lives as a site for the expression of ritual, entertainment, family life, or work.

Finally, the Guide suggests a framework for exploring the associations, networks, institutions, and friendships which Jewish women have created throughout the course of their lives, particularly those with other women. Such relationships have often channeled the nature and direction of women's participation in social, cultural, and political arenas. The Guide helps narrators bear witness in their own terms to the major social and cultural movements and the economic and political transformations that they have lived through.

Thus the Guide's ten frameworks establish the important reality that women have been active agents and makers of history. In so doing, it helps frame the many connections between the experiences of gender and those of ethnicity, religion, and nationality, helping us to understand the diverse parameters of being American, female, and Jewish in different regions, in different epochs, and for women of vastly different backgrounds and personal histories. The Guide helps us understand that the personal lives of women have intersected with the historical events of their times in myriad ways.

Jewish women's oral histories greatly enhance the mission of the Jewish Women's Archive to "uncover, chronicle, and transmit" the rich history and legacy of Jewish women in North America. Through these inspiring testimonies, we become aware of how profoundly Jewish women have shaped the multifaceted worlds in which they live – and American Jewish experience as a whole.

We welcome you to this exciting endeavor of history-making!

# 1

# Conducting Life History Interviews

||||||||||||||||||||||||||||||||||||||||||||||||||||||||||||||||||||||||||||||||||||||||||||||||||||||||||||||||||||||||||||||||||||||||||

Top: Beatrice L. Levi, Bottom: Esther Eggleston

# Conducting a life history interview

can be a profoundly moving experience for both the oral historian and the narrator. It is also a complex process involving many detailed steps. Preparation is the key to success. In this section, we show you the essential components for every phase of the interview process.

## GETTING READY

### Choosing a narrator

Each of us has important stories to tell. Whether a woman is an "ordinary" person or someone who has had a demonstrable impact on her community or field, she can be a *narrator* — that is, the person whom you invite to share the story of her life through an oral history interview.

*Why do we use the term "narrator"?*

Over the past half century, as oral history and other ethnographically-based methods of collecting information have become widespread, a variety of terms — *subject, interviewee,* and *informant* among the most popular — have been used to denote the person who is being interviewed. We choose to use *narrator,* as do many oral historians, because it implies that the individual is actively involved in shaping the interview with the oral historian rather than simply responding to her questions. By recalling memories, allowing her mind to freely associate from one subject to the next, and *narrating* her life story, the narrator's role during the oral history interview is substantial.

*A special person in your life*

Many of us have a special person in our lives whom we would like to interview and whose voice we would like to preserve. Perhaps it is your mother or grandmother or another family member who is the bearer of tradition or the keeper of family memories and stories. Or it may be someone you saw as a role model or who had a major impact on your community. Because of your personal relationship to her and her significance in your life, she is a natural person to invite to participate in an oral history interview.

*Community oral history*

If you are planning, either by yourself or as part of a community group, an oral history project that will include the stories of many individuals, it is important to consider the qualities to look for in a potential narrator:

◆ The person is knowledgeable about the subject you are interested in exploring and can contribute an interesting perspective.

◆ The person is a good communicator who is able to tell her story effectively and fluently.

◆ The person is willing and able to participate in the project.

*Extending the invitation*

Whomever you invite to be interviewed, whether it is your grandmother or a prominent member of the community, it is important that you communicate your purpose, what you intend to do with the interview and who will have access to it, and what the narrator's rights and responsibilities will be throughout the process.

If you know your narrator personally, try to arrange a visit or phone call in advance so you can explain to her what is involved in a life history interview and answer her questions about the subject matter you are interested in or the kinds of questions you would like to ask.

For a community project, it is usually a good idea to communicate with a prospective narrator in person and then follow up with a letter specifying what the project is about and reiterating the main themes.

## Pre-Interview Questionnaire

Before you conduct an interview, prepare yourself as thoroughly as possible by learning about your narrator's background and the context — historical, political, social, and cultural — in which she has lived. Even if the narrator is your mother, grandmother, or another woman whom you know well, there are undoubtedly many things you do not know about her life.

The PRE-INTERVIEW QUESTIONNAIRE (PIQ) provides a snapshot of your narrator's life. A "just the facts, ma'am" document, the PIQ enables you to document names, dates, places, and key events in her family background; and information about her educational experiences, work history, places of residence, involvement in the community, and Jewish identity and affiliations. In addition, we ask the narrator to list three key topics that she would like to discuss during the interview.

Many oral historians believe that these questions provide the backbone for the interview, providing crucial information about what topics to cover. The PIQ also helps you think about what additional background research you may need to do so that you can ask informed questions. Finally, the PIQ provides a handy way to check the spelling of names and places, as well as the accuracy of information, when you are editing an interview transcript.

## Background Research

A critical step in the interview process is to conduct background research that will help you ask better and more informed questions. At JWA, we have found that it is important for the oral historian to have general knowledge about the historical context in which the narrator lived, as well as specific background information about her life.

There are many ways that you can learn about your narrator. If she is a well-known figure in your community or in a particular field of endeavor, you can search for information on the Internet. Local, regional, or even national archives may also contain information about your narrator, her family, or key events and institutions with which she was affiliated.

On a more general note, having basic knowledge of American Jewish history adds immeasurably to the oral historian's ability to ask insightful questions. Scholars interested in women's roles in the American Jewish community have produced an impressive body of work over the past several decades. We urge you to read some of the books and articles listed in the Selected Bibliography on American Jewish Women (see Appendix).

In addition, Jewish historical societies have a wealth of resources and information about the history of local Jewish communities or the activities of particular communal organizations and institutions. Your local library or synagogue archive may also have relevant information. Finally, the narrator herself may have articles, journals, letters, or other documents about particular events or activities that she would be willing to share with you.

Conducting research can sometimes seem like a daunting challenge. You may have limited resources and time constraints that dictate how much effort you can invest. In that case, even a brief period — a couple of hours — devoted to background research can enrich the interview experience for both you and the narrator.

## Developing Your Questions

Once you have completed your background research, your next task is to develop a set of topics and questions that will help you guide the interview. Knowing the right questions to ask — and how to ask them — are the fundamental skills you will need to conduct the interview.

In Part 2: JWA's Topic Guide for Life History Interviews, we provide a comprehensive framework of topics and sample questions that will allow you to explore many aspects of your narrator's life. In the section below, you will learn the basic rules for formulating good interview questions.

## Learning How to Ask Good Questions

Through years of experience conducting interviews, oral historians have learned a great deal about what kinds of questions elicit the richest stories. The general rule is that open-ended questions tap into your narrator's wellspring of memories, eliciting stories with a distinct voice and narrative flow. Closed questions, on the other hand, tend to result in brief, factual responses.

*Examples of closed questions include:*

- What year were you born?
- What were your parents' names?
- When did your family come to this country?
- What high school did you attend?

*Open-ended questions often begin
with the following words and phrases:*

- Why?
- Can you describe...?
- Tell me about...
- What was that like?
- How did you feel when...?
- What were your expectations about...?
- What challenges did you face when...?

It is not always possible to ask open-ended questions, and occasionally you do need to clarify a factual issue. In the one-two punch method, you ask a closed question to elicit a factual or specific response, and then follow that with an open-ended question that will allow the narrator to elaborate on her response.

| CLOSED QUESTION | OPEN-ENDED QUESTION |
| --- | --- |
| What was your mother's name? | Describe your relationship with your mother when you were growing up. |
| When did you move to the new house? | How did you feel about moving to a new house and a new neighborhood? Describe your experience. |
| When did you get married? | As a young woman, what were your expectations regarding marriage and how did that affect your decisions? |
| When did you graduate from medical school? | Tell me what it was like being one of three women in your med school class. |
| Did you attend services regularly when you were a child? | What role did synagogue attendance play in your family when you were a child? How would you describe women's roles in public worship at that time and how did you feel about it? |

**Bridal shop saleswoman Selma Litman with her wedding photos**

◇◇◇◇◇◇◇◇◇◇◇◇◇◇◇◇◇◇◇◇◇◇◇◇◇◇◇◇◇◇◇◇◇◇◇◇◇◇◇◇◇◇◇◇◇◇◇◇◇

## Interviewing Tips

Although it takes two to create an oral history, it is important to remember that the focus of the interview should always be the narrator's story and her experiences. This can sometimes be a challenge. Indeed, women's normal conversational style encourages us to show empathy with the other person by sharing similar personal experiences. Women also use a variety of verbal cues to indicate that we are paying attention to our conversational partner's story. Good oral history technique, however, requires that we find other ways to show support for our narrator. Here are some tips on good interview techniques:

◆ Don't be afraid of pauses or silences. Sometimes it takes a moment for the narrator to collect her thoughts.

◆ Don't interrupt your narrator with other questions while she is in the middle of a story.

◆ Do follow up with additional questions that probe a topic and allow your narrator to reflect more deeply on her experience.

◆ Ask questions about basic biographical information first to put your narrator at ease and help develop rapport.

◆ Resist the urge to give encouragement by interjecting "uh huh" "oh, wow," or other utterances. Instead show your appreciation or empathy through eye contact, facial expressions, and other non-verbal signs.

◆ Keep the focus on your narrator's story by stifling the urge to share your own experiences or feelings.

◆ Avoid leading questions that make assumptions about what your narrator thinks or feels.

◆ Conduct the interview in a place and time of your narrator's choosing. The more comfortable the narrator feels, the more likely she will relax and enjoy the experience.

◆ Make sure that there are as few extraneous noises in the environment as possible. The sound of ringing phones, barking dogs, fans, air conditioners, refrigerators, or other electronic equipment can generate intrusive background noise during the interview. Ask if you can unplug appliances for the duration of the interview.

◆ If possible, arrange the interview so that only you and the narrator are present. The presence of others can dramatically change the dynamics, content, and quality of the interview.

◆ Restrict any interview session to a maximum time of one and a half to two hours. For older people especially, fatigue can be a significant factor in their ability to remember and their overall experience of the interview. If necessary, schedule subsequent sessions as time and resources permit.

## Choosing Your Equipment

In preparing for an oral history interview, one of the most important, and confusing, issues we all face is what kind of equipment to use. With recording technology undergoing rapid and constant change, choosing your equipment can be a challenge. It is helpful to know that, even among experts, there is no clear agreement about what kind of equipment is best. For most of us, however, there are two key decisions that need to be made:

◆ Should I use audio or video recordings, or a combination of the two?

◆ Should I use analog or digital recording equipment?

What we present here is a very basic overview of some of the key considerations in selecting appropriate equipment for your project. The information is drawn from our own experiences as well as from websites and books on oral history (see APPENDIX). We also urge you to consult with people in your community who are knowledgeable about recording technology, and look at the myriad books, manuals, and websites that provide detailed descriptions and explanations of the options and technology currently available.

### Audio Versus Video Recording

It is helpful to think about the choice between audio and video recordings both in terms of its impact on the narrator and the ways in which you intend to use the interviews in the future. Video recordings have the obvious advantage of adding a rich visual dimension to the interview document by capturing the "look" of your narrator, her expressions and mannerisms, her body language, her personality. On the other hand, some narrators may feel uncomfortable and self-conscious about being videotaped, which can diminish your ability to put the narrator at ease and establish rapport with her.

Additional considerations about video recordings are:

◆ Watching "talking heads" can be visually boring if the interview goes on for several hours. If you intend to produce a video as your final product, remember that you can also use still photographs, home movies, and archival footage, as well as images of objects, documents, and places to create visual interest.

◆ Video equipment can be more costly than audio equipment.

◆ Video recordings involve a substantially more elaborate setup than audio for lighting, sound, and set, and may require the presence of one or more "crew" during the interview session.

◆ Both the narrator and the oral historian may feel less at ease on camera.

Some oral historians are ardent champions of video over audio recordings, while others take the opposite position. One option that many oral historians prefer is to audio record the initial interview and then follow up by recording selected stories on video.

For JWA's *Weaving Women's Words* project, we decided that our elderly narrators would be more at ease with audio recordings. In a few cases, we videotaped an additional session. At the same time, we hired a photographer to make intimate and evocative portraits of each narrator, thus providing wonderful visual material for our project.

## Analog Versus Digital Recording

One of the most important decisions you will have to make is the choice between quality analog or digital equipment for audio and video recording. The differences between the two essentially have to do with the ways in which they record sound:

◆ Analog tape recorders, such as cassette tape recorders, use magnetic tape to record sound.

◆ Digital machines use software programs and hardware to record sound by compressing the data into more compact forms.

Budgetary concerns often drive decisions about what equipment to choose. Analog recorders are often less expensive than digital, and the tapes can easily be transferred to digital formats at a later time. Many people also find cassette tape recorders more familiar and thus easier to operate.

Digital recordings, on the other hand, allow you to edit the recordings more easily and to make them accessible via the Internet. Another important consideration is that there is no loss of quality when you create duplicate copies of the interview. The main disadvantage of using digital equipment is that you cannot rely on particular software or hardware for any length of time because of changing technology and, in many cases, built-in obsolescence.

## Harpist and champion of the arts, Bernice Rind

*Equipment Primer*

Here are some of the key considerations in choosing and operating different types of equipment:

CASSETTE RECORDER:

◆ Choose the best quality, the lightest weight, and the most durable recorder you can afford. Make sure it has the following features:

◆ Digital tape counter (for analog recording)

◆ Battery power and recording level indicators

◆ Jack for external microphone

◆ Usability with batteries and electrical adapter

◆ Keep the volume control in the middle range while recording in order to decrease background noise.

◆ Except in an emergency, use electric current rather than batteries during recording sessions.

◆ Use only top-quality, high-bias, 60-minute tapes. Longer tapes compromise the quality and durability of oral history recordings.

MINIDISC RECORDER:

◆ Minidiscs are popular among oral historians because they are small, easily portable, and produce excellent-quality sound recordings.

◆ Consumer models are relatively inexpensive.

◆ Make sure that your minidisc has microphone inputs.

Hand-held, high-quality microphones may need a pre-amplifier to work with a minidisc.

◆ A standard minidisc records 74 minutes of sound. You can increase this up to 148 minutes of acceptable quality speech, which may be important during an interview.

MICROPHONE AND HEADPHONE:

◆ For better sound quality, always use an external microphone rather than the recorder's internal one. Many oral historians use an *omnidirectional* microphone, which is helpful if either the narrator or oral historian move their heads or body positions during the interview. Another option is a lavaliere microphone that you can attach to the clothing of both the narrator and the oral historian. This type of microphone picks up rustling of fabric, however, and needs to be carefully monitored through good headphones, which should be worn throughout the interview.

◆ A solid, sturdy microphone stand with adjustable clips and arm is useful so you don't have to hold the mike.

VIDEO RECORDER:

◆ Digital video has become the medium of choice for oral history video recording. In contrast to videotape cameras, digital cameras can be used under more varied conditions with excellent results.

◆ The sound quality of digital video compares favorably with that of digital audio recordings.

◆ Digital video is easy to use, reproduce, and edit. Multiple copies can be dubbed without loss of quality over generations.

◆ Use a boom or lavaliere microphone for the best sound quality.

◆ Many oral historians recommend creating a backup audio recording of the interview.

PRACTICING ON YOUR EQUIPMENT:

The watchword is practice! Whatever recording equipment you ultimately choose, it is important to become thoroughly familiar with its operation before you go into the interview. Not only will you make fewer mistakes that can undermine all your efforts; you also will put your narrator at ease if you look like you know what you are doing.

## Release Forms

One of the most important steps in preparing for the interview is creating an appropriate release form that establishes the rights and responsibilities of each of the participants. We strongly recommend that you consult the Oral History Association's booklet, *Oral History and the Law* by John A. Neuenschwander, to learn about the ethical and legal issues involved in oral history (see SELECTED ORAL HISTORY RESOURCES).

At JWA, because of our commitment to providing a strong ethical and legal framework for our oral history work, we have developed a two-step process for obtaining permission from the narrator.

## Preliminary Release Form

Before the start of the interview, we ask the narrator to sign a PRELIMINARY RELEASE FORM. At that time, we go over the form with the narrator to ensure that she understands the terms of the agreement and that she is comfortable with the process. (See sample release forms in the APPENDIX.)

For JWA's *Weaving Women's Words* oral history project, the preliminary release form:

◆ establishes that the interview is part of a broad, national oral history project

◆ states the narrator's consent to be interviewed

◆ gives JWA the rights to the oral history

◆ states that JWA intends to use the collected oral histories for a variety of purposes in a variety of formats

◆ establishes the narrator's rights to review the transcript and impose any restrictions she desires on access to the audio recording or the transcript

## Final Release Form

JWA's policy is to return the transcript to the narrator for her review following initial editing. Although this involves extra effort and time on our part, we believe that the narrator should have the opportunity to read the transcript and feel comfortable about releasing it for use. The FINAL RELEASE FORM provides an opportunity for narrators to indicate any restrictions they would like to place on release of the interview. Such restrictions may include:

◆ Eliminating passages or restricting access to certain sections of text

◆ Restricting access to certain categories of individuals

◆ Establishing a time frame for release of the interview (for example, five years from the date signed on the release form or after the narrator's death)

◆ Requiring written permission for access

◆ Restricting release of the audio recording unless it matches the approved, edited transcript

## Interviewing relatives and close friends

Even if you plan to interview someone close to you, we suggest that you go through the process of explaining your purposes for conducting the interview and what you intend to do with the interview. Before you share your mother's views on life and family, it is helpful to make sure she understands who will eventually have access to her stories. Knowing what you plan to do with the interview may indeed influence her decisions about what stories she wants to tell. This, we believe, is her right as a narrator. We all have more than one way of formulating our life story, and who the intended audience is has a lot to do with how we construct the narrative at any particular time. If possible, it is a good idea to draw up a *simple release form* that describes what your goals are for the interview and how you intend to use it in the future.

## Setting Up the Interview

After all the work of preparing for an interview, the best-laid plans can be seriously undermined by not paying sufficient attention to the interview setting. The best space is one in which your narrator feels comfortable and you control the environment in order to avoid interruptions and background noise.

### Selecting a space

Although some interviews take place in an office or studio, narrators often feel most at ease in their own homes. When you are ready to schedule the interview, ask your narrator where she would prefer to do it. If possible, check out the space in advance. Otherwise, explain to her the kind of environment required for a good interview — quiet and away from potential interruptions — and ask her about the space she suggests.

In general, make sure that the space offers comfortable chairs for you and the narrator, a table or stable surface for your equipment, access to electrical outlets, and means to control the noise level in the room.

### Setting up

Set up your interview space so that you are sitting approximately four to six feet from your narrator. Not only will this provide conditions for optimal sound recording, but it will help you to establish and maintain good rapport with the narrator throughout the interview. She will be able to hear you comfortably, and you will be able to maintain eye contact with her. It is also a good idea to have a table near you where you can put your recording equipment, topic/question guide, notepad and other materials.

Place your equipment on the table for easy access. You need to be able to see the recording meters and how much tape is left on analog recorders, as well as to be able to change tapes or discs with minimal interruption during the interview. If you are using an omnidirectional microphone, it is helpful to put a pad beneath it to reduce vibrations. Whenever possible, use an electrical outlet to plug in your recording equipment and reserve batteries for emergency use. This way, you won't have to worry about batteries running out during the interview.

### Positioning the microphone

Because an oral history interview is an interaction between you and the narrator, it is important that the equipment record the dialogue between you. This means that you should position your microphone(s) so that both of your voices can be recorded clearly.

An omnidirectional microphone will pick up sound from both of you. Position the microphone two to three feet from the narrator, pointed in her direction. It is helpful to carry a microphone cable with you in order to position the microphone properly.

If you are using a lavaliere mike, clip one on your narrator's clothing approximately 10 inches from her mouth, and another mike on your own clothing.

Before you begin the formal interview, do a quick sound check. It is often helpful to ask the narrator to state her name and address as a way of checking the sound levels. You can then record the opening announcement in order to check your own voice.

# DURING THE INTERVIEW

After all your preparations, you are finally set up and ready to begin. The next section provides essential steps to take during the interview process.

## Establishing Rapport with the Narrator

An important component of a good interview is the rapport you establish with your narrator. The good news is that life history interviews by nature generate empathy and forge bonds, even between strangers. Your interest in your narrator and your attentiveness to her stories are key to building rapport.

Talk to your narrator while you set up; informal conversation helps to put people at ease. Just steer clear of subjects that can segue into interview territory. There's nothing worse than hearing your narrator "spill" a terrific story – off mike. In most cases, the second rendition is never quite as rich or as fresh. Therefore, it is best to stick to neutral chitchat.

Make sure to let your narrator know that you can stop the interview at any point if she gets tired or needs to take a break. For many people, especially if they are older, an hour and a half to two hours should be the maximum time for an interview session.

Finally, and most importantly, be an attentive and responsive listener. Use eye contact and other non-verbal means to communicate your interest and appreciation.

### DON'T LEAVE HOME WITHOUT IT
◆ Recording equipment
◆ Topic/question guide
◆ Notepad
◆ Pen or pencil
◆ Extension cord
◆ Adaptor for electrical outlets
◆ Microphone cable
◆ Additional tapes or discs
◆ Batteries for recording equipment
◆ Release form

# Recording an Opening Announcement

Prior to starting the interview, make an opening announcement on your tape or disc. This ensures that anyone listening to the interview in the future will have the basic information about when, where, and with and by whom the interview was recorded.

Include the narrator's name, your name, the date and location of the interview, and if applicable, the name of the project and the organization for which the interview is being recorded. A typical announcement might be:

> "This is (*your name*) and I am here with (*narrator's name*) to record her life history as part of the (*project title*) of the (*organization*). Today is (*date*) and we are at (*place/address*)."

In some states, you must also record an oral agreement with the narrator stating that she agrees to be interviewed and understands that the interview is being recorded. For JWA's *Weaving Women's Words* project in Seattle, for example, a typical announcement was:

> "This is Roz Bornstein and I am here with Louise Azose to record a life history interview with her as part of the *Weaving Women's Words* project of the Jewish Women's Archive. Today is Tuesday, May 23, 2002, and we are at Louise's house on Mercer Island, Seattle. Louise, do I have your permission to record this interview with you?"

For every subsequent tape or disc, you need to record an opening announcement. For example:

> "This is Roz Bornstein, and this is the second tape of my interview with Louise Azose on Tuesday, May 23, 2002, at her home on Mercer Island, Seattle. This interview is part of the Jewish Women's Archive's *Weaving Women's Words* project. Louise, do I have your permission to continue taping this interview?"

## Ask Easy Questions First

Narrators often find it easier to start by answering easy questions first. Because most people feel relatively comfortable talking about their family background, many oral historians proceed chronologically, beginning with questions about the family's arrival in America followed by those relating to the narrator's childhood memories. Leave more controversial questions until later, when you have established rapport with your narrator and she has become more comfortable speaking candidly with you.

## NOISE TO AVOID

- Ringers on telephones
- Open windows
- Fans, air conditioners, and heaters
- Chiming clocks
- Televisions and radios
- Background music
- Pets
- People in the environment
- Interference due to rustling fabric (when using a lavaliere mike) or noisy nervous gestures (worry beads, shaking ice in glass, pounding the table, rustling papers, etc.)

## Dealing with Difficult Subjects

Every life has its share of difficult topics that a narrator may or may not want to share in an interview. You may know about aspects of your narrator's life – either through the Pre-Interview Questionnaire, research, or personal knowledge – that you suspect she may be reticent to discuss. Depending on her personality, generational experience, or life circumstances, for example, she may be more or less comfortable talking about issues regarding her sexuality, health, or marital status. Or there may be difficult issues that she or her family have had to contend with.

By asking pertinent, broad-based questions in a sensitive manner, you can open the door to difficult topics. Whether and how she will respond, however, is for the narrator to determine.

It is also helpful for narrators to know that they will have the opportunity to review the interview transcript, and delete or restrict sensitive sections that they may not wish to make available.

Finally, before publicly releasing an interview, be sure that you understand the fundamental issues regarding your own legal responsibilities and liabilities as oral historian. Statements in the interview that may be libelous should be brought to the narrator's attention and deleted or sealed.

## Obtaining a Signed Release Form

Before the end of the interview session, it is important to have the narrator sign the PRELIMINARY RELEASE FORM. We strongly recommend that you go over the form with the narrator and ask her to sign it before you begin the interview session. Without this signed document, you will not be able to use or release the interview, no matter how wonderful it may be.

If you are using a two-part release process, as JWA did for *Weaving Women's Words*, you can remind the narrator that she will have an opportunity to review the transcript and make any changes or corrections she thinks are necessary before the interview is released. At that time, she will be able to stipulate any restrictions regarding the use of her interview.

## Completing the Proper Word Form

Especially if you are planning to have the interview professionally transcribed, it is very helpful to fill out a PROPER WORD FORM. This form provides a list of correct spellings for all proper nouns, such as places and names, in the order in which they occur during the interview.

If the narrator has used foreign language, it is also helpful to include transliterations of all non-English words. Remember that even if these words or phrases seem common to you, they may be completely unfamiliar to a professional transcriber. To reduce the number of corrections that will be necessary during the editing process, include any words or names that you know may have several possible spellings.

Some oral historians jot down words to check as the narrator uses them. To avoid distracting the narrator or interrupting the flow of her story, we generally do not recommend asking her how to spell something during the interview; rather, wait until the end of the session or another time to ask how to spell the words on your list. You may also use the PRE-INTERVIEW QUESTIONNAIRE as a spelling reference for place and proper names.

Another common practice is to compile the PROPER WORD FORM by listening to the interview. Although time consuming, many oral historians find this useful to prepare for follow-up interview sessions, both to determine which topics they may want to revisit or probe and which new topics or directions to explore.

## Protecting the Tape or Disc

After you finish recording a minidisc or cassette tape, you should immediately follow these safety precautions to prevent accidental recording over the interview: If you use a minidisk, move the white button on the upper-right corner. If you use an audiocassette tape, punch in the two tabs.

Right after the interview, label your tapes or minidiscs. At a minimum, you should include the narrator's name and the date of the interview. If you used more than one tape or disc during the interview session, include that information on your label. For example, if you used two tapes during a session, common ways to label them are 1(2) and 2(2) or "1 of 2" and "2 of 2".

**Dorothy Franco Muscatel, a vibrant social organizer in Seattle**

# AFTER THE INTERVIEW

Although it may seem that the most important phases of conducting an oral history are the pre-interview preparation and the interview itself, good stewardship requires that you complete the following post-interview tasks to ensure the preservation and accessibility of your interview. Otherwise, it may end up gathering dust on a shelf.

## Saying Thank You

Sharing one's life story is an act of generosity. Whether your narrator is a member of your family or your community, a colleague, or a public personality, it is considerate — and standard interview protocol — to let her know that you appreciate the time she has given you and, more importantly, the memories, wisdom, and reflections she has shared. A note of thanks is always appropriate and welcome, whether the oral history is an independent endeavor or part of a larger project.

## Interview Logs

Access is one of the two main goals of the post-interview phase. The INTERVIEW LOG provides an easily scanned, chronological summary of the interview contents and where to find specific information in the interview (see the sample INTERVIEW LOG in the APPENDIX). This log is an important tool for ensuring the accessibility and utility of the interview, whether you make a verbatim transcription or not.

Content tags in the log should flag and summarize facts, names, stories, and events. These tags should be descriptive and succinct. The point is to identify a topic without going into details; if the reader wants to know what was said, he or she can go to that point in the interview.

If you do not have a transcript available, you will need to start by listening to the recorded interview from start to finish and jotting down key names, topics, events, and stories. Look at the counter on your recording equipment to note where each topic occurs. (Note that these counter numbers will only serve as approximate time markers; every machine runs differently.)

Make sure that you have a notation for at least every five minutes of listening time, unless there is one extremely long, coherent story that cannot be broken down into logical segments. Once you have a rough outline, go back and refine the list of topics, making sure that you have an accurate counter number for each.

If you have a transcript available, your first step should be to read through it, looking for notable topics, names, stories, and events, as well as keys to your narrator's attitudes about her life and the world. Make notes in the margins; these will be helpful references later when you listen to the audio recording and type up the log.

Log notations do not need to be complete sentences. Some examples of tag phrases include:

- ◆ Attitudes towards...
- ◆ Discussion of...
- ◆ Memories of...
- ◆ Story of...
- ◆ Explanation of...

Below are examples of Interview Log notations from a *Weaving Women's Words* interview:

| COUNTER TIME | NOTATIONS |
| --- | --- |
| 12:29 | Family: Relationship with sister Beverly and family leisure activities; story about mother's *pushke* box; relationship with parents; father, a tailor, made all her clothes; fashion/style then and today |
| 18:40 | Parents' work: father, a tailor, and mother worked in department store; mother encouraged Shirley to become pharmacist to support herself |
| 20:38 | Life in Portland, Oregon, as a child |
| 22:18 | Neighborhood: Growing up on First Hill in Seattle — a Japanese neighborhood at that time; grandfather held property of Japanese tenants during internment; reflections on Japanese internment era and relations |
| 24:03 | Jewish home life and education: keeping kosher, Temple de Hirsch (Reform); Depression; Jewish community in Capitol Hill neighborhood; expectations re: Jewish associations; family involvement in Workmen's Circle; Alts Farm/commune, where liberal Jewish community summered; Yiddish-speaking immigrant parents |
| 32:26 | Education at Broadway High School: clubs; relationships with women; class; relationship with Jewish women and non-Jewish friends in high school and today. |

## Transcribing and Editing

*Creating the transcript*

When it comes to transcription, oral historians have differing views; virtually all of them, however, agree that written transcripts provide the quickest and easiest means of access to the recorded interview. We strongly urge you to transcribe the interview yourself, or if possible, hire a professional transcriber, preferably someone who is experienced with oral history methods of transcription. Ask around for recommendations.

As a general rule, an hour of tape will take approximately four or more hours to transcribe. Before you enlist the services of a transcriber, ask to see examples of her work and about her fees. Remember that people don't talk like they write;

our speech is full of um's and uh's and false starts and pauses. Be sure to discuss with the transcriber how you want to handle such idiosyncrasies – that is, to include them or not. (While there are arguable reasons to preserve every utterance made by your narrator, they clutter up a transcript and make it much more difficult to read.)

### Editing the transcript

Transcribing the interview, even if it is done professionally, is the first step in the process. The next is editing the transcript. While this is not essential, at JWA we have found that our narrators have been happier with the final product, and more likely to release their interviews, when we gave them the opportunity to lightly edit their words.

Language in its oral form is entirely different from the written. Because a transcript documents spoken words, no one expects the language to be grammatically perfect or polished. We do, however, recognize that narrators want to be represented to the public in a way that feels comfortable to them.

For our *Weaving Women's Words* project, we followed these procedures for ethical and legal reasons, but also to honor the wishes of our narrators:

1. **Transcript No. 1:** Each interview was professionally transcribed, using the PROPER WORD FORM as reference.

2. **Transcript No. 2:** The oral historian proofed and edited Transcript No. 1 while listening to the recorded interview.

3. **Narrator's review:** The narrator was asked to review Transcript No. 2, checking for spelling or factual errors. She entered her changes in the margin of the transcript. Along with the transcript, we enclosed two copies of the FINAL RELEASE FORM so the narrator could specify any restrictions on the release or use of her interview. She returned both copies to us to sign, and we returned one copy for her files.

4. **Final Approved Transcript:** We input the narrator's corrections and deleted any passages she requested be removed. This third version was the FINAL APPROVED TRANSCRIPT of the interview.

The Final Approved Transcript is the only written version of the interview that is released for use by researchers and the general public. In some cases, our narrators have also requested that the audio recordings of their interviews be restricted unless and until corrections and deletions can be made.

## Getting the Interview Out

Once you have finished processing the interview, many choices await as to what to do with the narrative you have created. In today's world of digital technology, there are virtually no limitations on the shape of your final product. At JWA, for example, we give each narrator a bound, archival-quality copy of her narrative along with a CD of the recorded interview. You can easily add a visual dimension to your "book" with scanned photographs or other relevant documents.

When possible we encourage you to deposit a copy of your Final Approved Transcript and audio recording in a local archive. If you are participating in a community oral history project, make provisions for preserving copies of the interviews in a reputable archive or library where researchers and community members will have access to these stories. For a smaller project involving an interview with an individual, ask your synagogue or local historical society if they would like a copy for their collection.

There are many additional ways to bring your work to the attention of a larger community. Books, documentary films, radio series, websites, public presentations, performance pieces, and exhibitions are excellent creative outlets for showcasing oral history.

At the Jewish Women's Archive, we developed community-wide exhibitions based on the oral histories we collected in Boston, Baltimore, and Seattle. Each evolved into an innovative format developed by community members to honor their narrators. Depending on the community's resources and desires, each exhibition combined stories with photographic portraits, works of contemporary art, and personal artifacts and memorabilia. You can view an online version of the exhibits in Seattle and Baltimore at our website (www.jwa.org).

More than a single life history of an individual, your narrator's story belongs to the larger narrative of the American Jewish experience. In the future, scholars will look to oral histories like the one you have created for insights into the realities of women's lives at the turn of the twenty-first century. What were the concerns of American Jewish women? How did they manage their multiple roles as mothers, wives, breadwinners, and activists? How did their expectations evolve as women's roles changed – in the workplace, within community organizations, in the home, in places of worship? How did their energy and commitment help shape our world?

The oral history you create today will be among the primary sources that may help to answer these and other questions, and serve as a window on these lives and times.

## Pioneer businesswoman in residential real estate, Fiola Blum

# 2

## JWA's Topic Guide for Life History Interviews

# The heart of a good interview

is the dialogue between the oral historian and the narrator. Unlike a memoir, an autobiography, or a journal, all products of a single sensibility, an oral history is generated by the interaction between the participants, each of whom plays a distinct role in the process. The oral historian creates a supportive space in which the interview takes place, provides the conceptual framework, and guides the interview by asking considered questions and by listening well and with sensitivity. In response, the narrator taps her memory and reflects on the people, places, and events that have shaped her personal history and composed her life story.

JWA's gendered approach to life history interviews offers women a unique opportunity to think and talk about their own experiences as American Jewish women. This Topic Guide consists of ten broad frameworks as approaches to a woman's multifaceted life. Each represents a significant aspect of her experience and offers an entrée into her story.

In preparation for conducting a life history interview, it is important to understand the historical context in which your narrator has lived. Each framework section opens with an introductory essay by a leading scholar to provide a perspective on the subject and how it relates to the life experiences of American Jewish women. You will also find a list of key topics discussed in the section followed by sample questions on a range of related subjects. Finally, we include exemplary quotations from JWA's oral history archives. These brief vignettes will give you a sampling of the diverse times and places in which our narrators have lived and the variety of evocative stories that women share through oral history.

# Using the Topic Guide

One of your most important tasks is to prepare a set of questions and topics that will guide the interview. On the following pages you will find hundreds of questions about every aspect of Jewish women's lives. Not all of the questions will be relevant to the life history of any one individual narrator. Rather, the topics and sample questions should be used as suggestions; feel free to make up your own questions or to customize ours. As oral historian, you will decide which topics are most appropriate for a particular interview and narrator.

As you study the frameworks and questions, consider what you already know about your narrator. Review her completed Pre-Interview Questionnaire for an overview of times, dates, places, and major events or experiences in her life. For example, did she have a career that is central to her sense of identity? Did volunteer work or community activism play important roles in her life? Has your narrator been married or in a long-term relationship? What is her educational background and training?

As you read the introductory essays, think about how historical context helped shape your narrator's life experience. What were her expectations about career and family? How did being a woman shape her experiences in the workplace, in her community, and within her family? What impact did being Jewish have on her values, her life choices, and the options available to her? How did the places she lived affect the course of her life? What impact did major national and international events and movements have on her experiences and her sense of self?

Drawing on what you know about your narrator and her life, consult the Topic Guide for subjects you might want to cover in the interview and questions you might wish to ask. For each framework, we have included a Notes section where you can jot down your ideas. Most oral historians find it useful to make up in advance a list of topics and questions to bring to the interview so you won't forget anything.

As the interview proceeds, listen attentively to your narrator's words – and nuances. It is helpful to jot down on your notepad additional questions or subjects you may not have thought of previously. If you conduct more than one interview with a narrator, you will want to review the content of prior sessions to know which topics to pursue or revisit.

Above all, enjoy the dialogue and getting to know your narrator through the unique process of oral history.

Sephardic matriarch Louise Azose in her living room

# family

BY PAULA E. HYMAN

*I remember, as a child, living on Eager Street where we had horses and wagons and a big open courtyard. Growing up with your parents busy in the bakery every minute of the day and busy with babies, you really do get lost, unless you are able to work your way through it. The only time we ate together was Friday night or Passover, the Seder. Fridays we closed before the Sabbath started. For dinner, my mother made gefilte fish and chicken. Shabbos was wonderful. It was the only day my mother didn't work.*

**Rosalie Silber Abrams**

We are all born into families — families that seek to provide for their children's physical and moral sustenance and also to shape them in their own image. Whether mother and father ultimately succeed in their goals, children acquire their basic values and their sense of security from this first social unit that they encounter. Families are intermediaries between the individual and the larger society. When children feel the need to rebel, it is often against the family and what it has come to represent to them.

In virtually every culture, women's experience has centered on the family, even though in most societies women are not confined to the home. Household management long has been their responsibility; in the past two centuries in the West, home and family have been seen as the domain in which the woman's voice was meant to be clearly heard. It fell to women to set the moral and spiritual ambience of their homes and to teach the fundamental ethical and religious values to their children.

Members of the modern Jewish family shared many of these assumptions about family functioning and gender roles. But in some ways Jews had to expect more from their families than did others of various social classes. Mothers had to prepare their children to withstand social discrimination and to succeed in a broader society that did not fully welcome Jews. Families bore the main burden of providing the foundation of a religious and ethnic identity that would not be reinforced by public institutions. Until recent decades, many American Jews were children of immigrant parents. That fact simply exacerbated the intergenerational conflict that erupts in all families.

# family

Most importantly, Jewish families in the modern period have placed a premium on success, both material and intellectual. In part, the drive for their children's success was a way for Jewish parents to disprove the inferiority that the larger society imposed on Jews and to justify the sacrifices that were involved in international migration. And in part, it stemmed from a traditional Jewish culture that prized intellectual liveliness and verbal quickness, at least among males. Both traits were central to entry into the ranks of the learned elite.

It's hard to explore the Jewish family in contemporary America. American Jews contend with two stereotypes of Jewish families, even though they are contradictory. One presents a nostalgic, romanticized image of the Jewish family as a warm and ever supportive unit, often described as the haven from the storms that buffeted the ghetto. That family has no room for dysfunction and abuse. The second, popularized by American novelists, television script writers, and comedians, satirizes the Jewish family as too intense, too guilt-ridden, and too controlled by a domineering female. That family has no room for contentment and unconditional love.

Our task is to dig beneath the stereotypes to bring to light how American Jewish women today experience their families — the ones in which they grew up and the ones they have formed. How have their families contributed to the construction of their self-understanding, their values, their choice of activities, and their Jewish identity? Was growing up female in a Jewish family a source of empowerment or of struggle? In an era when Jews are more like their neighbors than ever before, what, if anything, is distinctive about the Jewish family?

The family is ever changing in its structure but it still faces the tasks of sustaining children and transmitting values to them. Jews in contemporary America feel less of a need to prepare their children for a hostile society, but their families remain the major socializing agents of their children. And the family is still the central, though certainly not the only, site of women's experience.

# Sample Questions

## FAMILIES OF ORIGIN

◆ Which of your family members settled in the United States? Where did they come from? What were their motivations?

◆ Describe your grandparents. What was your relationship with them? What influence did they have on your life?

◆ Where and when were your parents born? What do you know about their childhood and early adulthood? Describe your parents' respective roles in your home and family life (including religious, educational, and work).

◆ Where and when were you born?

◆ Do you have siblings? Where and when were they born? Describe each of them briefly and your relationship to them.

◆ Describe any unique circumstances in your early family life (adoption, illness or death of a parent or sibling, parents' separation or divorce, child of survivors, etc.)

◆ Where did you grow up? Describe your house and your neighborhood. Who lived in your household?

◆ Who were the significant adults involved in your upbringing (parents, grandparents, step-parents, adoptive parents, other relatives or non-family members)?

◆ As a child or young woman, did you consider your mother a role model? Your father? Why or why not? Were there other family members who served as role models for you?

◆ Were girls and boys treated differently in your family? Explain what you believed your family's expectations were regarding education, marriage, work, Jewish identity, and religious observance.

◆ Describe your relationship with your extended family.

## MARRIAGE

◆ What messages did you imbibe from your family and community regarding marriage?

◆ How did Jewish cultural and religious values and expectations impact your experiences and attitudes?

◆ How and when did you meet your husband?

◆ Describe your courtship, wedding and honeymoon.

◆ What were your expectations of marriage during the early years of your marriage? How did these expectations change over time?

◆ Describe your roles and those of your husband within your marriage. For example, what were your respective responsibilities regarding childrearing, household finances, and social activities? How did these change over the course of your marriage?

◆ If your marriage ended, did you enter into a new relationship? With whom? What were your expectations and attitudes about roles within your new relationship?

◆ Describe your experience of separation and/or divorce, or widowhood.

◆ If your marriage ended and you then remained single, describe your experiences as a single woman.

## COMMITTED RELATIONSHIPS

◆ If you formed a long-term partnership with a man or woman outside of marriage, describe your expectations, commitments, and respective roles within the relationship.

◆ What were your family's attitudes toward your relationship?

◆ How did societal expectations and norms affect your relationship?

◆ How did Jewish cultural and

religious values and expectations influence your experiences and attitudes?

◆ How did you meet your partner? Describe the early stages of your relationship.

◆ Did you formalize your relationship? If so, describe.

◆ Describe your roles and those of your partner within your relationship. For example, what were your respective responsibilities regarding household responsibilities, household finances, and social activities? How did these change over the course of your relationship?

◆ What were your attitudes towards having or adopting children? Childrearing? If you had children from a previous marriage, describe how this impacted your relationship.

◆ If your relationship ended, did you enter into a new relationship? With whom? What were your expectations and attitudes about roles within your new relationship?

◆ Describe your experience of separation or life after the death of your partner.

◆ If your relationship ended and you then remained single, describe your experiences as a single woman.

## SINGLE WOMEN

◆ If you have remained single throughout your life, describe your experience. Was this a conscious choice? What factors influenced your decisions?

◆ How did your family's attitudes and societal expectations affect your experience?

◆ Describe your relationship with other family members. Did you develop particularly significant relationships or roles with other family members (siblings, parents, nieces and nephews)?

◆ How did your feelings and attitudes about remaining single change over time? What factors, personal and societal, influenced your perspective?

◆ How did Jewish cultural and religious values and expectations influence your experiences and attitudes?

◆ What were the particular

# family

challenges and joys you experienced as a single woman?

## CHILDREN AND CHILDREARING

◆ As you were growing up, what were your expectations and attitudes towards having children? As an adult?

◆ If you have children, how many children do you have? When were they born?

◆ Describe any significant childbirth experiences.

◆ Do you have children in your family who are not your biological children? Are they adopted? Stepchildren? Other?

◆ If you have adopted children, how and why did you decide to adopt? Describe your experience of adopting a child.

◆ If you have stepchildren, how old were you and they when they became part of your family? Describe your experience of being a stepmother.

◆ How did you and your husband/ partner share childrearing roles and responsibilities?

◆ Did any other adults have a regular role in rearing your children (for example, a grandmother, aunt, nurse, nanny or housekeeper)?

◆ How would you describe yourself as a mother? Do you think of yourself as permissive, flexible, strict, protective, overprotective? Why?

◆ What rules did you establish regarding your children's behavior?

◆ What values did you try to inculcate in your children? How did you do this? What do you think are the source of these values in your life (for example, American, Jewish religious or cultural, regional)?

◆ For you as a parent, how important was transmitting Jewish values and rituals? How did you and your husband/partner accomplish this?

◆ What, if any, were the major conflicts between you and your husband/partner regarding childrearing?

◆ How do you think your children might describe your parenting?

◆ How do you think your childrearing style compares with other mothers of your own generation?

◆ Did your style of childrearing differ from that of your own mother? How? What did you want to emulate? Change?

◆ If your children are parents, how does their childrearing style compare to yours?

◆ What activities did you and your child or children particularly enjoy doing together?

◆ Describe a typical day in your household when your children were young or adolescent.

◆ If you do not have children, was that a choice on your part? What has been your experience of being childless?

◆ If you have experienced the death of a child, how has this affected you?

## GRANDPARENTING

◆ What were your expectations about becoming a grandmother?

◆ How many grandchildren do you have? What are their ages?

◆ Was your own mother (or someone else) a role model for you as a grandmother? Why and how?

◆ What did you want to be called as a grandmother? Why? What associations does this name have for you?

◆ Describe your experience of being a grandmother. What have been your roles and responsibilities? Greatest rewards or problems?

◆ How have changing roles and expectations for seniors affected your experience of being a grandmother?

◆ What impact has the increased mobility in American society had on your relationship with your grandchildren? If your grandchildren live far away, how do you sustain your relationship with them?

◆ How often do you and your grandchildren tend to see each other? Under what circumstances (daily life, holidays, vacations)?

◆ Do you have great-grandchildren? If so, describe your experience. How does being a great-grandmother differ from being a grandmother? What is your relationship with your great-grandchildren?

**Seattle dressmaker Carolyn Danz with her granddaughters**

## notes

Teacher Nina Lederkremer in the classroom

# education

BY PAMELA S. NADELL

*Clipping from the Hopkins newspaper: "Eleven under-graduate men accepted to the medical school" — with last names in alphabetical order. And then at the end of the alphabet it says, "Miss Finkelstein." I wasn't even allowed into their alphabet.*
**Dr. Ruth Finkelstein**

The Talmud teaches, "A person who has knowledge has everything" (Nedarim, 41a), and America's Jewish women have long taken that lesson to heart. The great letter writer of colonial Jewry, Abigail Franks, saw to it that her daughters learned French, Spanish, and Hebrew, along with needlework and the harpsichord. Years before founding the National Council of Jewish Women in 1893, Hannah Solomon joined the Chicago Women's Club, which required its members to read Plato, St. Augustine, and Karl Marx as part of a curriculum of self-education. Education was so important to the budding East European Jewish immigrant writer Mary Antin that she lied about her age in order to attend Boston's public schools. And in 1903, the forty-two-year-old Henrietta Szold, the future president of Hadassah, enrolled in the Jewish Theological Seminary, determined to get an advanced Jewish education.

Over the course of the twentieth century, America's Jewish women continued to pursue education with a passion. As Frieda M. reminisced in Sydney Stahl Weinberg's *The World of Our Mothers*, "We were poor, but my father had a thing about education. He said to all of us, 'I can't give you beautiful things, but as long as you want to go to school, you can go to school'" (New York: Schocken Books, 1988, p. 167). Some took a path from grammar school to high school to college just so that they could return to those same classrooms as teachers. Others stopped along their way to study Judaism in temple Sunday schools or the *alef-bet* in congregational Hebrew schools. Especially in the latter half of the century, many new venues and opportunities arose for formal and informal Jewish education. All of them — Jewish day schools and university curricula, youth groups and summer camps, education-oriented trips to Israel and Holo-

# education

caust-related activities — expanded Jewish learning opportunities for young people.

But for many women, education is a lifelong passion. Throughout their lives, they have found new places and spaces for learning. As Jennie S. recalls in *The World of Our Mothers*, "I go to lectures, I listen…and I learn" (ibid, p.182). Twentieth-century — and twenty-first-century — American Jewish women find a dazzling array of lifelong educational possibilities. There are lectures sponsored by Sisterhood Shabbat and workshops at Hadassah's annual convention. Elderhostel offers programs in Jewish spirituality and history. Women of all ages study for their bat mitzvah while feminist seders introduce unsung heroines. Book groups read and discuss new Jewish writers, and you can sign up to receive a daily e-mail on ancient rabbinic texts.

The opportunities for learning abound. America's Jewish women have seized them with a passion and thirst that make education, including Jewish learning, a major theme in their lives and their history.

# Sample Questions

## GENERAL EDUCATION

◆ As a child, where did you go to school?

◆ What school experiences stand out as being most formative? What classes did you enjoy most? What did you enjoy least? Why?

◆ What extracurricular activities were you involved in and what drew you to them?

◆ Describe the experience of being Jewish in your school.

◆ Describe the experience of being female. Were girls treated differently than boys?

◆ Describe the social life in which you and your friends participated.

◆ Did you feel part of the mainstream in your school? Did you consider yourself "popular"? What did that mean?

◆ If you felt "different" in your school environment, what were the sources of these feelings (i.e., being an immigrant child, difficulties with speaking English, learning issues, standards of attractiveness or beauty, sexual orientation, few other Jews)? How did you cope with feeling different?

◆ Did you have any particular role models, male or female, in school, such as teachers, coaches, or adult advisors to extracurricular activities? Describe your relationship with them

and their impact on your life.

◆ Describe any educational experiences outside of school that were important to you as a child (i.e., camp, classes, clubs).

◆ Can you think of any books that you enjoyed reading during your school years? Magazines? Other cultural influences?

◆ What did you want to be when you grew up? Why? Were there careers or professions of interest that you did not feel were open to you as a Jew or as a woman?

## POST-SECONDARY EDUCATION

◆ What were the expectations and standards in your family regarding post-secondary education? Were there differences for sons and daughters?

◆ If you didn't continue your education, was that a choice on your part? How did you feel about it?

◆ If you continued your education beyond high school, how did you choose what school to attend?

◆ What were your personal goals for your education? Looking back, how would you evaluate your experience overall?

◆ What were your most important classes and activities? Describe.

◆ Did you have a mentor or favorite

teacher? What impact did she or he have on your life?

◆ What was your college major and how did you choose it?

◆ Do you think that females had a different educational experience than males? Describe.

◆ Describe any graduate or professional training you had. How did being a Jewish woman influence your choice of profession?

◆ Did being a woman or a Jew pose any particular challenges in your field of study? What impact did it have, if any, on the training you received?

## JEWISH EDUCATION

◆ What formal Jewish educational experiences did you have as a child?

◆ What were your most and least favorite subjects?

◆ Were girls treated differently than boys? Explain. How did you feel about that?

◆ How useful was your Jewish education to you? What did you learn that feels significant to you? How do you feel about your Jewish education in retrospect?

◆ Were there any significant Jewish learning experiences you had outside of a school setting as a child

(i.e., camp, youth movement, clubs)? What impact did these experiences have on your life? On your knowledge or understanding of what it meant to be Jewish? To be female?

◆ Describe the social life in which you and your friends participated. In what ways, if any, did your social life revolve around your synagogue or Jewish school community? Around formal or informal Jewish educational experiences such as camps or youth movements?

◆ How did your own Jewish educational experiences affect the choices you made for your children?

## LIFELONG LEARNING

◆ Have you participated in formal or informal education classes as an adult? In what contexts? What drew you to them? Describe your experiences.

◆ What impact, if any, do you think Jewish feminism has had on your desire to learn more about Jewish religion, culture and history? Have you taken any steps to augment your Jewish education as an adult?

◆ Did any of your educational experiences make a lifelong impact? If so, which ones?

# education

# notes

Painter and sculptor Amalie Rothschild in her studio

# work

BY HASIA DINER

*When I went to work, no woman in our strata of society worked because they wanted to work. And it took a certain kind of husband to encourage you to do that. I've been working forty-five years now, and I'm so glad. Life is so much richer.*
**Lois Blum Feinblatt**

◇◇◇◇◇◇◇◇◇◇◇◇◇

*I loved to teach. This was my life. My husband said to me, "When you come to Chizuk Amuno Congregation, you're like a mezuzah. Everybody kisses you."*
**Nina Lederkremer**

◇◇◇◇◇◇◇◇◇◇◇◇◇

For American Jewish women, like women everywhere and throughout history, work has been a constant factor in their lives. They may not have drawn a paycheck or earned money in their own right, but they have worked in their homes — as daughters, sisters, and wives — cooking, cleaning, and raising children. It is the labor of women that sustains the flow of daily life.

Historically, Jewish women's paid work in the United States falls into several categories. First, Jewish women worked in enterprises that grew out of their roles within their families and homes. From the middle of the nineteenth century into the second decade of the twentieth, Jewish immigrant families took in boarders to provide extra income. Women managed the work involved with boarders by cleaning and cooking, providing the needed services for the paying customers.

Secondly, Jewish women historically have played a crucial role in small businesses, both in large cities and small towns. Throughout the sweep of American Jewish history, stores of various kinds functioned as the backbone of the Jewish economy. These stores relied on the labor of women, usually the wives, who stood behind hundreds of thousands of counters, interacted with customers, stocked the shelves, and dealt with wholesalers. Jewish shopkeepers and their families typically lived above or behind their store. This reality fused Jewish residential patterns and Jewish entrepreneurship, creating little separation between the home life of Jewish women and their work experiences.

In some cases, however, Jewish women went far beyond simply "helping out" in these stores. While it was the men who were customarily regarded as the owners, there are well-documented accounts of indepen-

# work

## PAID WORK

## UNPAID WORK WITHIN THE HOME AND FAMILY

dent women entrepreneurs who established and managed their own enterprises of various sizes and with varying degrees of success.

In the late nineteenth and early twentieth centuries, many single, Jewish-immigrant women — and later their American-born daughters — worked in the needle-trades industry as sewing-machine operators in sweatshops and in larger factories. They also found employment as glove makers, milliners, and garment workers. As an influential labor force, they played a major role in trade-union activities and contributed many leaders to the women's trade-union movement.

Typically, Jewish women employed in industry would leave their job once they were married, returning only in the event of a family tragedy, such as the death of their husband. Not so their daughters, however. Born and educated in the United States, these women moved into new professions such as teaching, library work, and social work during the second and third decades of the twentieth century. In the process, they found ways to combine work and family. These women viewed their work not only as personally fulfilling and well-paid; they also believed that they performed a crucial public service, particularly as teachers.

Jumping forward one generation, we see yet another work transition among Jewish women who came of age after World War II. They benefited from the opening up of higher education to women and the breaking down of barriers against Jews and women. In large numbers, these women entered the most prestigious professions available in American society: academia, medicine, and law. In the generations that followed, Jewish women's work lives have been profoundly shaped by the feminist assault on male privilege, and Jewish women have benefited at every level by the opening up of doors once closed to women and to Jews.

# Sample Questions

## PAID WORK

◆ As a young woman, what expectations did you have regarding your working life? If you chose to work or not to work in paying jobs, what factors influenced your decisions?

◆ How have your attitudes towards women's participation in the workplace changed over time?

◆ What factors influenced your choice of profession or particular jobs? What responsibilities did you have in your various jobs?

◆ What factors determined changes in your jobs or career path?

◆ Did you work continuously in a specific job or career? For how long? Did you work continuously after your children were born? If not, describe your patterns of work.

◆ Did you do any work from your home? Describe.

◆ What were your goals and aspirations regarding your work life?

◆ Did you anticipate or experience any obstacles or challenges because of your gender or religion? How did you handle these issues? Were there other factors that presented particular obstacles or challenges to you (i.e., Jewish religious observance, sexual orientation, physical disabilities)?

◆ Were your aspirations and abilities taken seriously? What opportunities existed for advancement?

◆ Did you feel that being a woman presented obstacles to advancement in your work environment? Was it an advantage?

◆ Did you ever experience sexual harassment or sexual discrimination on the job? If so, describe.

◆ Did you ever join a union in your workplace? Describe your involvement.

- ◆ Did you have any mentors or role models in your work life? If so, what role did they play?
- ◆ What was your best experience as a working woman?
- ◆ What rewards did work provide?
- ◆ What dissatisfactions, if any, did you experience in your work?
- ◆ What was your worst experience as a working woman?
- ◆ Was there a women's work culture in your working environment that you can describe?
- ◆ What were your expectations around earning money? In your first jobs? In later jobs?
- ◆ How did you and your husband/ partner allocate roles and responsibilities concerning family finances? Has this changed over time?
- ◆ In what ways did your own work contribute to your organization or business?
- ◆ In what ways did your work contribute to your family's income and lifestyle?
- ◆ How did you balance your roles and responsibilities on the job and within your household?
- ◆ What do you consider to be your greatest achievements in your field of work? What are you most proud of?

## UNPAID WORK WITHIN THE HOME AND FAMILY

- ◆ How were household responsibilities allocated in your home? How did being a Jewish woman influence your expectations, and those of other members of your household, about who was responsible for what tasks?
- ◆ What were your major responsibilities within your home? Did they change during the course of your marriage/relationship?
- ◆ Who was responsible for the care of children in your household? For elderly family members? For those who were ill or disabled?
- ◆ How did you feel about the roles that you played and/or were expected to play?
- ◆ How did your expectations about your role(s) and those of other family members change over time?
- ◆ What impact, if any, did the feminist movement have on your expectations, and those of other family members, regarding allocation of roles and responsibilities?

# notes

_____
_____
_____
_____
_____
_____
_____
_____
_____
_____
_____

Bernice Stern, first woman to serve on King County Council

# community service

**BY DIANNE ASHTON**

*In 1953 I urged the school I worked in to integrate our faculty. The Brown v. Board of Education decision had just been made. By '55, I was president both of the Montrose school board and the Barrett school board, which had two schools — one for black girls and one for white girls. I integrated the two schools and they built a whole new school.*

**Clementine L. Kaufman**

olunteerism encompasses a broad range of ideas and activities linking women. Women volunteer in many ways, from giving their time, money, or skills to donating their possessions to recruiting friends and family members. And they volunteer for many reasons and causes, from the purely personal and pragmatic like sharing day-care responsibilities, to the lofty and idealistic like fostering world peace.

Duties vary as widely as goals. Working a regular shift in a thrift shop that donates its profits to a community service agency, for example, might require a volunteer with business skills. On the other hand, a woman who volunteers to mobilize support for peace, women's rights, or Israel would need experience as a political organizer and activist. Yet, each of these different efforts may express a worldview that shapes the meaning of life and of Jewishness for the women who join up.

Volunteerism can offer women a door to a world beyond the home. Some women have dedicated their lives to that larger world, creating veritable careers for themselves through voluntary organizations. This was especially true for women of earlier eras who were barred from meaningful paid labor. Such women often created new associations: Hannah Greenebaum Solomon and Sadie American together established the National Council of Jewish Women in 1893. Henrietta Szold created Hadassah, the women's Zionist organization, in 1912. Through these and other national organizations — founded for charitable, educational, religious, or political reasons during the first few decades of the twentieth century — women working in local groups across the country shared ideas and resources and understood their own needs by comparing them to similar situations faced by women nationwide.

Throughout the twentieth century, Jewish women were also linked

VOLUNTEERISM

MOTIVATIONS

ORGANIZATIONAL
CULTURE

nationally through their local synagogues. Organizations like the National Federation of Temple Sisterhoods (now the Women of Reform Judaism), the Women's League for Conservative Judaism, and the Women's Branch of the Union of Orthodox Jewish Congregations provided similar kinds of assistance to synagogues throughout the United States. Although barred from both the rabbinate and cantorate until 1972, Reform Jewish women became influential in synagogue life by managing gift shops, assisting religious schools, and providing programming for members. Both Reform and Conservative women promoted change in synagogue life by pooling their efforts and ideas at both a local and national level. Women's participation in synagogue-based groups increased in the post World War II era, which saw a boom in new synagogues as Jews relocated to the suburbs in many areas of the country.

Many women see volunteer work as an extension of their domestic life, rather than as a doorway to the world. They donate cookies to bake sales, clothing to rummage sales, or toys to day-care centers. And they pay their dues and assist in solving any crises that may arise. No matter how dedicated and capable an organization's leader might be, no group can be effective without the labor of myriad women like these. While these busy women might be able to volunteer little one year, they might shoulder more significant burdens and leadership roles at another time in their lives. Although they may see their service as insignificant, volunteerism is a way of life whose rhythms ebb and flow, and these women are the very backbone of the organizations they support.

# Sample Questions

## VOLUNTEERISM

◆ Have you served as a volunteer for any community or civic projects? In the Jewish community? Elsewhere (e.g., League of Women Voters, alumni groups, cultural, artistic or political organizations)?
◆ Which organizations have been most important to you? Describe your involvement.
◆ What roles did you play within the organizations for which you volunteered?
◆ What was the impact of your work within the organization?
◆ What impact did the organization and its activities have on your community?
◆ How have your volunteer activities changed over time? What factors have influenced these changes?
◆ How did you balance your community work with your family obligations?
◆ How did you balance it with paid work?

## MOTIVATIONS

◆ What were your motivations for undertaking volunteer work? What did you hope to accomplish?
◆ Did world events or events within your own community affect your decision to get involved?
◆ What factors influenced your choice of organization or level of involvement? Did you have role models who influenced you?
◆ Do you think of yourself as a leader? As an activist?
◆ Did you have any mentors? Were they male or female? What did you learn from your mentors?
◆ Do you associate particular Jewish values, such as *tzedakah* or *tikun olam*, with the work you did?
◆ Do you associate particular American values with your work?

## ORGANIZATIONAL CULTURE

◆ Can you describe the culture of the organization in which you worked

— for example, the status of women vis-à-vis men within the organization, the relationship between Jews and non-Jews, or the relationship between lay leaders and staff?

◆ Were there opportunities for advancement and personal growth for volunteers within the organization?

◆ How did being a Jewish woman affect your involvement?

◆ What were your satisfactions and rewards from this community service? What were the major problems you confronted?

**Dorothy Wittenberg serves lunch for low-income residents**

## notes

Seattle community historian Meta Buttnick blesses the candles

# Jewish identities

> *My mother — and I think all Jewish women — took a chicken and made twelve different dishes out of it. You made the soup, and then you roasted the chicken, and you chopped the liver. They took that neck skin and they stuffed it with flour and pepper, and sewed it up and roasted it with the chicken. I'm telling you — twelve different dishes.*
>
> **Selma Litman**

**BY KARLA GOLDMAN**

Understanding the place of religion in the life of an American Jewish woman may require consideration of a wide range of possible practices, beliefs, observances and experiences.

It is important to remember that women whose lives spanned the twentieth century have seen great changes in the possibilities for their own involvement in American Jewish religious life. Oral histories offer an opportunity for women to reflect on their changing roles in public worship and family celebrations and to examine how they have defined themselves in terms of their religious choices.

Different women in your family or community may have grown up in widely varied religious contexts. For some, childhood memories may revolve around their family's rejection of a religious Judaism. Others will remember an intensely lived religious culture where Jewish law governed most aspects of life. Many will recall religious practices that immersed women in the preparations necessary for offering kosher food and meals for family celebrations that were central to daily life and/or weekly Sabbath and holiday observances throughout the year. Some will emphasize synagogue-based activities like religious or Hebrew school and attendance at religious services. Among all these women, many will also associate Jewish identity with the politics, talk, and gatherings of their extended family.

For many American Jewish women, marriage and starting a family also meant making their own choices about the kind of religious life they

# Jewish identities

wanted. Those who grew up in immigrant households often saw setting up their own home as a way to establish themselves and their children as true "Americans." Women's religious choices may have been influenced by their spouse's background, by the kind of community they lived in, or by the opportunities they sought for their children. Their decisions have often been extremely important in defining the Jewish experience of their families and their communities. Much can also be learned about the American Jewish community from exploring what choices were available to women who did not marry or have children, or who were divorced or widowed.

In recent decades, American Judaism has been deeply transformed by evolving expectations for women. Consequently opportunities for involvement in public Jewish life will have changed greatly in the lifetimes of the women you will interview. Expansion in Jewish women's religious roles can be tracked across the twentieth century through the introduction of innovative ceremonies and roles for women.

The formal religious education of many women will reflect the expectations of their eras, families, and communities. Expanding educational and worship opportunities for girls, however, helped to open the way for greater women's involvement in Jewish liturgy and leadership. In 1922, Mordecai Kaplan, the founder of the Reconstructionist movement in Judaism, conducted a bat mitzvah for his daughter as a parallel to the coming-of-age bar mitzvah ceremony celebrated by thirteen-year-old Jewish boys. By the 1940s, bat mitzvah ceremonies had become relatively common in the Conservative movement, although the emphasis in Reform congregations remained on co-educational confirmation services until the 1960s. By the 1970s, bat mitzvah had generally become indistinguishable from the bar mitzvah ceremony celebrated by boys in the Reform, Conservative, and Reconstructionist communities.

Older women grew up in a Jewish world very different from today's. By the 1920s, women's organizations had become central to the social and cultural life of American synagogues of every denomination. These groups offered women avenues to engaged communal participation and leadership, even as they were excluded from general religious and institutional leadership. These groups remained quite important through the Depression, World War II, and the era of suburbanization that transformed many congregations in the 1950s and 1960s.

The rise of feminism in the 1960s and 1970s and women's changing roles in American society found strong expression within institutional Judaism, reflected in such innovations as the rise of the egalitarian bat mitzvah. The first American woman rabbi was ordained in 1972 within the Reform movement. She was followed by others within the Reform, Reconstructionist, and Conservative movements. Many women assumed prominent roles within their congregations as they moved beyond women's groups to fill general leadership roles including that of synagogue president.

The increasing presence of female spiritual and lay leaders has helped to expand the possibilities for all American Jewish women. Even among the Orthodox, recent decades have brought a transformative explosion in the opportunities for serious Jewish study now available to women and girls. Narrators may have experienced these changes in their own lives or through the lives of their daughters, granddaughters, relatives, or friends.

It is important to remember that the momentous individual experiences that embody these religious and societal changes, even if experienced by thousands of women across North America, could easily disappear from the historical record. For this reason, gathering women's stories about their educational and religious opportunities is critically important in piecing together the broader story of American Judaism during the twentieth and the beginning of the twenty-first centuries.

# Sample Questions

Jewish
identities

IDENTITIES

PUBLIC RELIGION

DOMESTIC JUDAISM

OBSERVING
LIFE-CYCLE EVENTS

## IDENTITIES

◆ How would you describe yourself in terms of your Jewish identity?

◆ How important is your Jewish identity to you?

◆ Have your feelings about being Jewish changed over time? How?

◆ What aspects of Jewish identity are most important to you (i.e., religious beliefs and observance, affiliation with a particular religious movement, relationship to Israel, secular Jewish culture, Yiddish culture, Sephardic culture, Jewish foods and culinary traditions)? How is this expressed in your life?

◆ How has being a woman affected your sense of yourself as a Jew?

◆ If you are a Jew by choice, describe your experience of conversion and of being a Jewish woman.

◆ If you (or members of your family) are married to a non-Jew, how has the experience of intermarriage affected you?

## PUBLIC RELIGION

◆ Growing up, did your family belong to a synagogue? If yes, describe your experience within the synagogue.

◆ Have you belonged to a synagogue as an adult? If yes, what was your involvement in the life of the synagogue community?

◆ Do you identify with a particular Jewish religious denomination or type of observance? If so, which one and why? Does this represent a change over your lifetime for you or your family?

◆ Did you raise your children with a religious orientation different than the one you grew up with? How and why?

◆ How do you feel about women's roles in public worship? How has your thinking evolved over time? What factors have influenced your thinking?

◆ Describe your own participation in public worship. Have you taken leadership roles in your community? Been called to the Torah for an *aliyah*?

Chanted Torah or Haftora? Presented a *dvar torah* or sermon? Led services?

◆ Do you cover your head or wear a *tallit* during public worship? Why or why not?

◆ Do you think that women rabbis and cantors are making a difference in their congregations? What is unique or special about their role or impact, in your experience?

◆ Did/do you participate in specifically women-centered prayers, rituals, or observances in the synagogue or other public settings? Describe your motivations and practice. For example, did you go to the *mikveh*? Have you participated in *Rosh Hodesh* groups? Women's *tefilah* groups? Describe your experiences.

◆ Have you been called to the Torah as a bat mitzvah? As a child? As an adult? Describe the experience and its meaning for you.

◆ Can you recall any milestones or turning points in your religious life?

## DOMESTIC JUDAISM

◆ In your childhood home, did your family keep kosher? Describe how decisions were made regarding *kashrut* and your family's practices. Did these practices change over time?

◆ Describe your attitudes and practice regarding *kashrut* in your home as an adult.

◆ Who prepared food in your family? Did you have any help in the kitchen?

◆ How did you learn to cook?

◆ What role do cookbooks play in your culinary knowledge and traditions?

◆ Do you have any special family recipes? Do you associate them with particular holidays, events or people? Do you prepare them any differently from your mother, grandmother or other relative?

◆ Were there any regional influences on the foods prepared in your home?

◆ What Jewish holidays did your family celebrate? Which were the

59

# Jewish identities

IDENTITIES

PUBLIC RELIGION

DOMESTIC JUDAISM

OBSERVING
LIFE-CYCLE EVENTS

most important?

◆ Did your family observe Shabbat? If so, describe how it was observed and the preparations made by you and others in your family. How have women's roles changed in how your family has prepared for and observed the Sabbath?

◆ Did your family observe Passover? What preparations were made in your home for the holiday?

◆ What specific roles did you and other women in your family play in preparing for the holiday? What roles did men play?

◆ Describe your family Seder. What roles did men, women and children play in your celebration?

◆ Have you or other women in your family ever led a Seder?

◆ Have you ever participated in a women's Seder? Describe your experience and its importance to you.

◆ What were your family's attitudes towards and/or observance of Christmas and other non-Jewish holidays?

## OBSERVING LIFE-CYCLE EVENTS

◆ What are the most important life-cycle events in your family?

◆ Describe how you celebrated or marked the birth of your children.

◆ Did you celebrate your children's coming of age with a bar or bat mitzvah ceremony? A sweet sixteen party? Describe the events and your feelings about them.

◆ Were these events marked in your own life? How did you feel about that?

◆ Has your family observed the Jewish rituals of mourning when family members have died? Have there been different roles for men and women during the funeral or the *shivah* period? If so, how has this affected you?

◆ Have you created and/or participated in new life-cycle events (e.g., to mark the beginning of menstruation or menopause; events related to women's reproductive lives, such as infertility, miscarriage, or still birth; commitment ceremonies or marriage with a same-sex partner; experiences of illness)?

## notes

**Baltimore community leader and activist Jane Krieger Schapiro**

# Jewish identities

IDENTITIES

PUBLIC RELIGION

DOMESTIC JUDAISM

OBSERVING
LIFE-CYCLE EVENTS

*Friday night, my mother made it a must. It's traditional with Jewish families, but with my mother, she didn't take 'no' for an answer. You knew you couldn't make any plans. Friday night was family night. It wasn't because they were religious, because my father did drive. But Shabbes was important as far as family togetherness, and it was stressed so much to all of us in the family that I did the same thing. Thursday, the baking started in our house. I can still smell the aromas of my mother's home, really, of all the cooking, and everything was home-made. I didn't cook like my mother did. I bought rib roasts — something that I never had in my parents' house, plus a chicken, always a chicken. And I baked apple pies and lemon meringue pies, and all the children and grandchildren's favorite cake on their birthday. If you ask my grandchildren about growing up, they will remember Friday night dinner and what I made as more important than anything about me.*

◇◇ **Elsie Miller Legum**

Alice Siegal with her great-grandmother's cooking utensils

# home and place

**BY JENNA WEISSMAN JOSELIT**

*My life was pretty protected. We didn't wander too far from the compound. Somebody asked my son Larry, when he was around seven or eight, if he thought that there were more Jewish people in the world or more other people. He thought about it and he said, "Well, I guess there are more Jewish people." So the person asked why he thought that and he said, "Well, in my family everybody's Jewish, in my Sunday School everybody's Jewish, and in my school almost everybody's Jewish. So yes, I guess there are more Jews."*

**Lois Blum Feinblatt**

Throughout much of the nineteenth and twentieth centuries, tradition and modernity, so often at odds with one another, heartily agreed on one thing: the role of the Jewish woman. Drawing on biblical imagery, some American Jewish leaders likened her to a "Priestess of the Jewish ideal and [a] Prophetess of Purity and Refinement," whose home was a "miniature Temple" consecrated to faith and family (Emil Hirsch, "The Modern Jewess," *The American Jewess*, Vol. 1, No. 1, 1895, p. 11). Others of a more ecumenical cast of mind allowed that the "Jewish ideal of womanhood is not the entrancing beauty of the queen of a knightly tournament nor the ascetic life of a virgin saint but wifehood and motherhood" (David Philipson, "Woman and the Congregation," *Proceedings, National Federation of Temple Sisterhoods*, 1913, p. 16).

In both cases, the Jewish woman was regarded as a paragon of domesticity who was most fully herself, and mostly highly valued by others, when attending to the needs of her household. This housebound view of Jewish womanhood transcended region, denomination, and even class, inspiring generation after generation of Jewish women to embrace it as their own. Even those who eagerly ventured outside the home to volunteer their time and talent at a settlement house or a synagogue sisterhood tended to see their communal work as an extension of their domestic duties and maternal sensibilities.

The domestication of Jewish womanhood saw its fullest and perhaps liveliest expression in the *Jewish Home Beautiful*, a popular compilation of songs, sayings, recipes, decorating tips, and tableaux vivant created in the early 1930s by Althea O. Silverman and Betty Greenberg. Going through eleven editions in less than twenty years, the book enjoyed middle-class, American Jewish women of the interwar period "to assume her role as

# home
# and
# place

## MIGRATIONS
## AND SETTLEMENT

## NEIGHBORHOOD,
## COMMUNITY
## AND REGION

## THE HOME
## AS FAMILY
## ENVIRONMENT

an artist, and on every festival, Sabbath and holiday, to make her home and her family table a thing of beauty as precious and as elevating as anything painted on canvas or chiseled in stone" (Betty D. Greenberg and Althea O. Silverman, The *Jewish Home Beautiful*, (New York, 1945, third edition, pp. 13-14)).

By likening the Jewish homemaker to an artist and her household to an artistic medium, the *Jewish Home Beautiful* recast the customary pieties about Jewish womanhood in a determinedly modern, even consumerist, idiom. As much a critique as a celebration, it spoke to the growing numbers of Jewish women who, throughout the interwar years, were beginning to look outside the Jewish community for affirmation, stimulation, and guidance. "Jewish mothers of today have not lost their desire to introduce beautiful pageantry into their homes." But instead of mining the "possibilities of our tradition," the text noted, they found inspiration in "strange sources" such as secular women's magazines and department stores. The *Jewish Home Beautiful* sought to rectify that situation by appealing to the senses rather than to the imperatives of Jewish history or tradition.

By the 1960s, however, the ideology of domesticity – once an article of faith – collapsed under the weight of feminism. More and more American Jewish women rejected its panoply of defined roles — Jewish woman as priestess, prophetess, wife, mother, and aesthete. No longer did they want to be confined to the home. What they wanted was to be citizens of the world.

At first the American Jewish community did not look favorably on the challenges and changes wrought by feminism. Eventually, though, as Jewish women came of age and consolidated their social, cultural, and economic gains, they generated a new ideology of Jewish womanhood, one that successfully reconciled the demands of domesticity and the claims of community with the possibilities of the self.

# Sample Questions

## MIGRATIONS AND SETTLEMENT

◆ Does your family have stories about life in the Old Country?
◆ How and when did your family arrive in the United States?
◆ What do you know about the circumstances of their journey and their arrival? Are there any stories about their early years in this country?
◆ Who in your family did not come to America? Do you know what happened to them?
◆ Are you and/or members of your family still in touch with relatives outside the United States?
◆ Has your family moved around within the United States? What were the reasons for the moves?
◆ Describe your experience of living in different parts of the country.

## NEIGHBORHOOD, COMMUNITY AND REGION

◆ Describe the neighborhood in which you grew up. What was distinctive about it?
◆ What was the ethnic character of your neighborhood? Did you consider it to be a "Jewish neighborhood"? What were its distinctive landmarks, including stores, places of worship, schools, etc.?
◆ Where would family and friends get together during your childhood and teenage years? Were there special gathering places? What would you do?
◆ Have you or your family experienced or been aware of anti-Semitism? How has this affected you?
◆ Are there special challenges to

being Jewish in your area of the country? Describe. How has it affected your sense of the larger American Jewish community?

◆ How has living in your region of the country affected the way you see or experience the world? For example, has living in your region affected your attitudes towards race?

◆ How has living where you do affected your self-perception, expectations, and behavior as a woman?

◆ Describe the nature of your interactions with Jews in your community. What were your interactions with people from other ethnic or racial backgrounds? Do you consider your patterns of relationships to be typical of others in your community?

◆ How has your city or town changed as a place for Jews to live over the course of your lifetime?

## THE HOME AS FAMILY ENVIRONMENT

◆ Do you consider your home to be a "Jewish home"? Explain.

◆ How does your home reflect who you are and what is important to you?

◆ Do you display or possess any objects, arts, crafts, or family heirlooms that mark your religious or ethnic identity? How does your home express your American identity?

**Community volunteer Magda Schaloum at home**

## notes

Passionate lifelong dancer Shirley Selis

# leisure and culture

**BY RIV-ELLEN PRELL**

All cultures have rhythms and all of us live our lives according to those rhythms. Not all days are the same and neither is time experienced the same within each day. Leisure is time outside of work. In some cultures the only leisure time was tied to a sacred calendar. In the modern world, leisure has been and remains a setting in which to experiment with new ideas and experiences.

Jews both pioneered the creation of leisure activities and were avid participants in them. For immigrants at the turn of the century, leisure served as an important vehicle for Americanizing, as well as for solidifying relations between Jews. But leisure, like work and family, was experienced differently by Jewish men and women.

Leisure time is usually shared with others. In contrast to Italians and Irish, for example, Jewish immigrants were more likely to spend leisure time with family members of both sexes, whether they went to the new silent movies in the neighborhood or gathered with their extended kin to pass the time. Immigrant Jewish families vacationed together, seeking relief from cities in the Catskill Mountains and later at the seashore.

In the same period, nevertheless, new leisure activities created a sphere available exclusively to young people, native-born and immigrants. Young Jews went to new amusement parks, dances, dancing schools, and soda shops with one another but never with their parents. Leisure taught them how to become Americans. Young Jewish women began dating in their leisure time, and ideas about "treating"

*When you are born to do something, it is never-ending. Regardless of how old you get, it is something that you have to do. And if you can no longer physically do it, you must be a part of it — whether it is going to performances, whether it is watching classes, whether it is guest-teaching, it is never ending. I stopped taking [ballet] class four years ago when I was eighty years old. I never for one moment felt embarrassed; sometimes I felt very honored. I would do something across the floor by myself, and they would all applaud and say, "That was gorgeous, Fuzz," you know? No, it doesn't end.*

**Shirley Selis**

◇◇◇◇◇◇◇◇◇◇

# leisure and culture

and sexual favors structured relationships between men and women during this period. Americanized and native-born Jewish women, when they had free time, also spent it in the company of other women. They played mah jong and card games, which often were condemned by rabbis and moralists. Women joined study circles and read about Zionism and Bible and Jewish history, often raising funds for philanthropy as part of these activities. In the early decades of the twentieth century, affluent Jews pursued other leisure activities. Jewish women organized charity balls and events. Early patrons of the fine arts, they also supported the creation of the Museum of Modern Art in New York as well as venues for modern dance.

Following World War II, the majority of Jews moved from the working class into the middle class. In the 1950s and 1960s, Jewish women with children tended to leave the paid workforce and became increasingly associated with leisure. In contrast to Jewish men, they devoted the majority of their leisure time to philanthropy, education, and volunteerism in synagogue and schools. Women also pursued activities associated with the suburbs, where many Jews had moved, but continued to go to the city in great numbers to participate as patrons of and participants in the arts.

Some of these patterns changed after the 1970s when Jewish women entered the paid workforce in unprecedented numbers. Increased work time took them out of the volunteer sphere and reduced their available leisure time. Increasing integration in the larger society has led Jewish women to move outside of exclusively Jewish venues for philanthropy. They also have increased their participation in sports and fitness, which was far less common during the first half of the century.

Leisure remains an important index of how Jewish women see themselves in relationship to work, the family, culture, and the larger society.

# Sample Questions

## VACATIONS AND TRAVEL

◆ Did your family vacation together? What were your favorite vacations?
◆ Did you attend summer camp? Was it a secular or a Jewish camp? How significant were your experiences at camp on your life?
◆ Have you been to Israel? When and under what circumstances? Describe your experiences and your relationship to Israel.
◆ Do you like to travel? Where have you gone? What do you like to do when you travel? What impact have your travels had on you?
◆ Does your family have a vacation home? When and how do you use it?

## HOLIDAY OBSERVANCES

◆ What American holidays were important to you (e.g. Thanksgiving, Fourth of July, Labor Day)? How did you celebrate them?
◆ Did you celebrate Christmas or other non-Jewish holidays? Describe your celebrations and the meaning of these holidays for you.

## FAMILY AND NEIGHBORHOOD PASTIMES

◆ How did you spend your leisure time as a child? As an adult?
◆ Which leisure activities were most important to you?
◆ Who did you tend to socialize with? Were your friends mainly drawn from within the Jewish community or from the broader society?
◆ How did you and your family spend time together on weekends?
◆ Did your family have reunions or family circles? How often and where would you meet? Was there a special program at these events? Who orga-

nized these get-togethers?

◆ Did you belong to any clubs or social groups (i.e., sororities, country clubs, Jewish community centers, *landsmenschaften*)? What role did they play in your life? In the life of your family and community?

◆ Did you participate in any informal neighborhood-based or social groups?

◆ Were any of these "women only" groups? Did they have a particular focus, such as playing cards, book groups, or groups for young mothers? Describe your involvement and the role they played in your life.

◆ How did you spend time with your women friends? What role did these friendships play in your life? Did these patterns change over time?

◆ How important were friendships with men in your life? Where did you tend to meet men who became your friends and what kinds of interests and activities did you share with them?

## ENTERTAINMENT AND SPECIAL INTERESTS

◆ Did you attend theater, dance, concerts, or movies? How important was this in your life? What did you most enjoy?

◆ Did you have any hobbies or special interests? Describe.

◆ Did you participate in community-based cultural events or performances, such as choruses or amateur theatrical groups?

◆ What role, if any, did sports play in your life?

◆ Did you have favorite radio programs or television programs that you or your family listened to or watched regularly? Describe.

## LANGUAGES

◆ What languages were spoken in your childhood home? Did members of your family speak Yiddish, Ladino, or other Jewish languages? Describe how these languages were used within your family.

◆ What languages did you learn in school? In other settings? Have these languages been important in your life? How?

◆ Do you enjoy Yiddish, Sephardic, or other types of Jewish films, theater, radio, or music? Do you have any favorite programs with Jewish characters or themes?

◆ What magazines or newspapers did you subscribe to? Describe their importance to you or other family members.

◆ How important was reading in your life? Where did you get books? What were some of your favorite books and authors?

◆ Did you belong to any book clubs? How were they organized and who participated?

# notes

"Mikveh lady" Cecilia Etkin by the ritual bath

# health and sexuality

BY BETH WENGER

*You had to be very proper. If a boy put his hands on your knee or in an embrace, that was not the proper thing. My mother put such fear in us. I fell in love my last year of high school — and really, to be a proper girl, I had to elope. But that wasn't unusual in our day. In my family, I'm number four that eloped.*

**Elsie Miller Legum**

Like other American women, Jewish women have experienced enormous transformations in their attitudes toward and experiences with sexuality and health over the course of the twentieth century. From the greater personal freedoms available to women in American society to the campaigns for birth control, to the contemporary struggles for abortion rights, Jewish women have been swept up in the rapid changes that have altered women's sexuality. At the same time, new medical discoveries have influenced the diagnosis and treatment of illness, while shifting family obligations have forced many women to assume new roles caring for family members. These and many other developments illustrate that women's private experiences of the body constitute a vital element in the narratives of Jewish women's lives.

As immigrants or the daughters of immigrants concentrated in urban centers, young Jewish women discovered unprecedented freedoms in America and imbibed all the pleasures of the city. Cities offered new spaces for socialization between the sexes — in dance halls, movie theaters, public parks, and amusement parks. Released from formal marriage arrangements, Jewish women dated freely and looked for romantic love when choosing their partners, even if they also desired economic security. Some women, such as the radical activist Emma Goldman who advocated free love, eschewed traditional marriage or heterosexual partnerships, but most simply looked to exert more personal choice in their relationships than might have been available to their immigrant parents.

# health and sexuality

## CHANGING ATTITUDES TOWARD SEXUALITY

## CHANGING ATTITUDES TOWARD HEALTH AND BEAUTY

## EXPERIENCES OF ILLNESS AND HEALTH

American Jews have consistently demonstrated a willingness to use birth control, relying on contraception and family planning to a greater extent than other Americans. Moreover, many Jewish women took active roles in the organized birth control movement and later pro-choice campaigns.

The structure of Jewish families reflected the general support for birth control. Jewish women tended to marry later than other American women. Once married, they managed their fertility with birth control and chose to have fewer children, patterns that continue to define Jewish families to this day.

Jewish laws and traditions influenced Jewish women's personal practices in a variety of ways. Historically only a minority have observed Jewish laws regarding family purity, abstaining from sexual intercourse during and for a few days after their menstrual periods and resuming sexual activity only after immersing themselves in a *mikveh* (ritual bath). Nevertheless, Jewish communities have continued to maintain *mikvehs*, and some Jewish women express a sense of personal empowerment through the observance of family purity. In recent years, new Jewish rituals and prayers have been created to mark key moments in women's reproductive lives, such as the onset of menstruation and menopause, as well as to mourn miscarriages or fertility problems.

Innovations in science and medicine have altered the choices available to Jewish women in childbearing as well as in other arenas of health. New fertility treatments now provide greater options to women who postpone childbearing or otherwise have difficulty becoming pregnant. Screening for Tay Sachs disease, for example, enables women to make choices, albeit sometimes difficult ones, about having children. On other medical fronts, however, they remain vulnerable: Rates of breast cancer among Jewish women, particularly of Ashkenazic background, continue to surpass that of most other groups of American women and remain a prevalent concern.

Jewish practices surrounding illness vary from traditional prayers recited at synagogue to personal prayers to the more recent innovation of Jewish healing rituals. Many Jewish women rely on prayer and community support when coping with their own illnesses. At the same time, like other American women, Jewish women have tended to bear primary responsibility for the care of family members during times of illness. With the increased mobility of American Jews, family members often live considerable distances from one another, placing additional strains on caregivers.

Jewish families and communities have become increasingly diverse and more accepting of various lifestyle choices. In recent years, lesbian, bisexual, and transgender women have created Jewish rituals and organized communities that embrace their choices and concerns. They have also redefined the traditional family structure to suit their needs and desires.

At the start of the twenty-first century, American Jewish women enjoy more freedom than ever before to express their sexuality, make informed medical choices, and control decisions about their own bodies. Although individuals, families, and communities continue to struggle with issues regarding health and sexuality, the future promises an increasing range of personal choices and the construction of more pluralistic families and communities.

*Aging is no fun, but you accept it. This is the way of life. Every life has to die, but I don't think about dying. I think about all the things I still have to do, all the things I still have to learn.* ◇◇ **Blanche Narodick**

# Sample Questions

## CHANGING ATTITUDES TOWARD SEXUALITY

◆ How do your views and your generation's views about sexuality compare with those of your parents' generation? Your children's generation?

◆ How did feminism and the sexual revolution affect your attitudes and your behavior?

◆ How did Jewish values affect your attitudes and behavior?

◆ Describe your attitudes towards homosexuality. How has your thinking about sexual orientation and sexual practice changed over time? What impact has the gay-rights movement had on you?

## CHANGING ATTITUDES TOWARD HEALTH AND BEAUTY

◆ Do you think that ideas about beauty and body image have changed over the course of your lifetime? How have they affected you?

◆ Were you aware of images in popular culture that were used to characterize Jewish women? How did these images affect your development and feelings about yourself?

◆ Describe your experience of growing older. What challenges have you faced and how have you coped with them? What sustains you through difficult times?

## EXPERIENCES OF ILLNESS AND HEALTH

◆ Have you or your relatives or friends experienced a serious illness, injury or medical condition that you would like to comment on? What impact did it have on your life?

◆ Were there certain beliefs and practices regarding illness and health that influenced your own behavior? What are the sources of these beliefs and practices?

◆ Are there specific Jewish values or practices that have influenced your attitude toward illness and health?

◆ Has the feminist movement affected your attitude toward women's health in general, or your personal health experience?

◆ Compare your views about general health practices with older members of your family or community. Describe the similarities or differences.

◆ In your family, what roles did women play in caring for ill or disabled family members? How did expectations of men's roles differ?

## notes

_____

_____

_____

_____

_____

_____

_____

_____

Visionary leader and activist Shoshana Shoubin Cardin

# women's identities

BY JOYCE ANTLER

*I became a public figure who wanted to teach women how to benefit from their rights when we would get them — not in a strident way, but in a sense of understanding that the average woman was going to outlive her mate. At that time she would have to function as an individual, independently. And in order to do that, she needed credit in her own name. She needed to be identified as an individual, not her husband's wife.*

## Shoshana Shoubin Cardin

One of the central themes in feminist scholarship has been the importance of the sense of community among women. As historian Nancy Cott noted in her book of the same title, "the bonds of womanhood" were a double-edged sword, constraining women but also empowering all-female friendship and social networks. Female friends, relatives, neighbors, and colleagues were integrated into a rich female culture that provided emotional supports and exerted social power, often working against patriarchal oppression. Women's "separate sphere" nonetheless encompassed many differences among women as well as collaborations with men belonging to their racial, ethnic, and religious groups.

Jewish women's friendships, social networks, and gender-specific communities established sisterhood as a leading dynamic in the lives of generations of women and the larger narrative of Jewish history. In traditional Jewish religion and culture, women were separated from men in the public space of the synagogue and in many of the public responsibilities of political and social life. While these demarcations would become less sharp over time in key denominations and American Jewish culture as a whole, sex-role differences continued to shape Jewish life in significant ways. Same-sex associations among Jewish women remained a powerful force in both private and communal life.

Jewish women encountered women who became their friends, colleagues, mentors, and role models in many different places: in garment factories, teachers' meeting rooms, and a variety of workplace sites; in women's clubs,

# women's identities

Sisterhoods, Haddassah and NCJW sections; in secular associations and movement marches; in schools, colleges, and reading circles; and through neighborhood, community and family gatherings, to name just a few. Grace Paley captured the importance of female friendship in her "Midrash on Happiness," where she wrote that what she meant by "happiness" was "three or four best friends to whom she could tell every personal fact and then discuss on the widest deepest and most hopeless level" the entire situation of the world. In the Jewish context, friendship provided personal comfort but also a way to understand – and often to impact – wider social circumstances.

The "bonds of sisterhood" that Jewish women shared with each other led to the first Jewish women's movement in the late nineteenth and early twentieth centuries, as "uptown" Jewish women came together to provide social supports for immigrants and to strengthen their own religious and educational affiliations. Jewish feminists also participated in the early American women's rights movement, advocating for the reform of marriage and property laws, woman suffrage, birth control, and improved conditions for working women. In later years, they championed the Equal Rights Amendment and other causes which fostered equal opportunities for women. Disproportionately represented in the leadership and rank and file of second wave feminism, Jewish women helped shape the revolution that changed the lives of millions of American women and their families. Within the Jewish community, they struggled to transform traditional male-dominated hierarchies of thought, worship, and action. Their challenges as feminists to both secular and Judaic patriarchal systems have been continual, effective, and creative.

Whether as friends, feminists, or members of close-knit sisterhoods, Jewish women have lived complex lives as members of multiple societies. Some, like Adrienne Rich, have felt "split at the root"– disconnected and fragmented; others have brought their multiple loyalties – as Americans, Jews, feminists or other kinds of citizen or cultural activists – into a harmonious, untroubled blend. Jewish women's identities vary according to region, education, economic, and religious background and a myriad of other factors. There is no one pattern that describes the variety of their associations, identities, and lifestyles. Yet their experiences have been important building blocks in the creation and expression of new traditions of female Jewish culture, out of which can arise new opportunities for defining roots, finding role models, and changing history.

# Sample Questions

## FEMALE FRIENDSHIPS AND NETWORKS

◆ How has your life been shaped by your friendships with women?
◆ Which female relatives were you especially close to while you were growing up? Describe your relationship with them and their influences on your life.
◆ Have you had lifelong or long-standing women friends? Describe the nature of those friendships.
◆ As an adult, are there activities that you do only with women friends?
◆ Are there times when you seek the advice of a woman rather than a man? Describe. Are there areas of your life that you have always shared with women and not men?

## IMPACT OF FEMINISM

◆ How would you define feminism or women's liberation?

- ◆ What are your attitudes towards feminism? Do you consider yourself a feminist? A "liberated woman"?
- ◆ At what point in your life did feminist issues become most relevant to you?
- ◆ How do your views regarding feminism compare with those of your mother's, children's, or grand-children's generations?
- ◆ How have your children's choices regarding work and family differed from yours? How do you feel about the personal choices your daughters, daughters-in-law, or granddaughters have made?
- ◆ Have you ever participated in an organized feminist organization? An informal feminist group (e.g., a consciousness-raising group)? Describe your experience.
- ◆ How has feminism affected your feelings about being a Jewish woman? What impact has Jewish feminism had on your self-image, beliefs, and practices?
- ◆ Were you ever aware of anti-Semitic or anti-Zionist attitudes within feminist organizations with which you were involved? If so, how did this affect your attitudes and involvement?
- ◆ Have you ever been involved with political movements that have challenged feminist programs or assumptions (i.e., anti-abortion campaigns, anti-ERA)?

## WOMEN AS ROLE MODELS AND CULTURAL HEROINES

- ◆ Have you had important female role models or mentors? How have they inspired and/or influenced you?
- ◆ Who are/were your favorite cultural heroines? What appeals to you about them?

FEMALE FRIENDSHIPS AND NETWORKS

IMPACT OF FEMINISM

WOMEN AS ROLE MODELS AND CULTURAL HEROINES

## notes

Social worker and homemaker Edith Furstenberg

# history and world events

BY REGINA MORANTZ-SANCHEZ

H istorians have not been trained to think of them-selves as actors in history. Traditionally theirs has been a self-effacing presence, commenting on past events rather than partici-pating in them. This has shifted to some extent during the last ten years as changes in the discipline have opened a space for using the personal voice.

Feminism's insight that "the personal is political" has helped to erode this artificial compartmentalization in the writing of history, and scholarly work has been particularly enriched. The 1950s, for example, is seen increasingly as a bifurcated time when public and private were severely split. I grew up in that era whose political world — shaped by the Bomb, the Cold War, debates over post-war welfare state entitlements, Brown vs. Board of Education, sit-ins, transformations in public under-standing of gender, sex roles and sexuality, and presidential elections — remained powerfully distinct from private life. That world was symbol-ized by the iconic white and democratic breadwinner family, which was safely ensconced in its well-accoutered suburban home. Like many girls, I struggled mightily with contradictory injunctions. I was to model my-self after June Cleaver, while competing academically with boys on equal footing and listening to rock music that subverted all accepted notions of female propriety.

Growing older has given me a past worth thinking about, and doing so has made me a better historian. But I've needed the past for another reason as well. When one of my daughters — the product of a Conservative

> The Center Club had a dining room where only men could eat. That was at lunch time. At night time, women could come in. So, we went. And we walked into the ladies dining room, and it was crowded. And the waiter said, "You'll have to wait for a half hour." And I said, "We don't have to wait for a half hour. That room in there is empty. There's hardly anybody in there." And he said, "But you're not allowed there." I said, "Okay." So I said, "Are you with me?" to my father and my husband and they said, "Sure." So we just walked ourselves into that dining room, and ordered lunch. Simple. We changed the rule.
>
> **Jane Krieger Schapiro**

# history
# and
# world
# events

IMPACT OF WORLD
EVENTS

INVOLVEMENT IN
POLITICAL PARTIES &
MOVEMENTS

REFLECTIONS

Jewish Day School and Hebrew-speaking summer camps — became a *Baalat Tshuvah* ["one who has returned"] at the age of fifteen, got married instead of attending college, and settled in an Orthodox neighborhood in Jerusalem, I needed history to make sense of her choices and my complex responses to them.

So I revisited my own Jewish self-construction in the 1950s. I understood at the outset that both my daughter and I lived in an era when choosing Judaism required conscious effort. But very different historical moments contributed to our choices, and that meant rethinking world-historical events in a way that could illuminate my own intersection with them. This is the task of oral history: It allows us access to the processes of our self-awareness, while providing a better understanding of how historical "conditions of possibility" limit and enable that self-understanding in myriad ways.

Measuring the similarities and differences in my own and my daughter's Jewish consciousness required an understanding of the impact of World War II on individuals, the post-war boom and its social, economic, and geographic consequences, the fascinating ecumenical reframing of American religious institutions after the war, the effects of Cold War ideology on gender and family roles, the post-1960s backlash against feminism and liberalism, the rise of the "unmeltable ethnics," and the realignment of political parties in the 1970s and 1980s. And that is just for starters.

For example, my parents were deracinated Jewish migrants to Los Angeles after World War II. They never would have left New York had my father not been wounded as a prisoner of war and ordered by his doctor to live in a warmer climate. Los Angeles was a city in enormous and vibrant flux where Jewish institutions, communal organization, and approaches to knowledge, ritual, and observance were being dynamically rethought. By luck my parents became involved in this buoyant era of institution building, involving me as well.

I had my own reasons for choosing Judaism, ones very different from theirs and much at odds with my daughter's twenty years later. I so loathed the female culture and role models pressed upon me by post-war prescriptions for American girlhood that I invented myself as a Jew in order to feel more comfortable with my outsider status.

For me, it was a fortuitous and rewarding espousal that molded me in ways I still esteem, but the Conservative Judaism I chose in the mid-1950s was not the Judaism my daughter encountered two decades later. Nor were the historical and personal inclinations behind my own engagement relevant for her, a product of the socially conservative atmosphere of the Reaganite 1980s. Indeed, my egalitarian and *halachically* inventive religious sensibility harbored too much uncertainty. Moreover, she doubted that feminist liberation was all it was cracked up to be; she saw that it could just as easily lead to divorce and single motherhood as to self-actualization and agency. Jewish feminism, egalitarian *minyans*, and the Conservative Movement's attempts at *halachic* modernization were not for her, a teenager navigating the troubled waters of sex, drugs, and rock-and-roll, and longing for certainty.

This is a story I cannot finish here. But hopefully it illustrates my point: Accessing the past through individual experience is a wonderful way to understand history, but only if we also probe how world events consistently shape our alternatives.

*We marched. We marched and we marched. We marched for everything that there was to march for that we thought important to our future lives.*

◇◇ **Beatrice L. Levi**

# Sample Questions

## IMPACT OF WORLD EVENTS

◆ As someone who has witnessed many of the key events of the twentieth century, which landmark events and social movements were most significant in shaping your life experiences and attitudes (e.g., the Depression, the Labor Movement, the world wars, the Holocaust, the founding of the State of Israel, McCarthyism, the Civil Rights movement, rise of feminism, gay rights movement)?

◆ What was the impact of the Holocaust on your personal and family life?

◆ Describe your relationship to Israel. Did you and/or your family support Zionism and the creation of the State of Israel? In what way? Why was it important to you?

◆ Have you visited Israel? When and in what context? Describe your reactions and Israel's significance to you?

◆ How would you describe the impact of feminism and women's changing roles and expectations on your own life? What is your opinion about women's changing roles?

## INVOLVEMENT IN POLITICAL PARTIES AND MOVEMENTS

◆ What political and social movements or causes have you been involved in? What were your motivations? Describe your experience.

◆ How did your religious, ethnic, or gender identity shape your experience within this movement? Did you face any particular challenges or obstacles as a woman? As a Jew?

◆ Would you describe yourself as an activist?

◆ Did you have role models who inspired you or influenced your own social activism?

## REFLECTIONS

◆ What are the most significant changes you've witnessed in your lifetime?

◆ How do you feel about the world today compared to the world in which you grew up?

◆ What have been the greatest advances you have witnessed in your lifetime?

◆ What trends or changes in the world are most disturbing to you? Why? Do you have a particular response or way of dealing with them?

◆ What words of wisdom would you offer to the generations that came after you? Do you have a philosophy of life or particular values that are important for you to share with your descendants?

◆ What are your most fervent hopes for the future?

## notes

_____

_____

_____

_____

_____

_____

*'My maternal grandmother came in 1913. She would always tell us stories, and we would say, "One more story, Grandma, one more story."*

Tillie Israel De Leon

# JWA'S GUIDING PRINCIPLES FOR CONDUCTING WOMEN'S LIFE HISTORIES

1. Ask questions that encourage your narrator to focus on her own experiences rather than those of other people in her life.

2. Explore family and cultural expectations that helped shape your narrator's life choices.

3. Provide opportunities for your narrator to reflect on changes in women's roles and status and the impact of these changes on her own life.

4. Explore particular challenges, obstacles, or advantages she faced as a woman.

5. Allow your narrator to follow the flow of her thoughts and freely associate from one story to the next.

6. Provide opportunities to discuss the interconnectedness of home, work, and community life.

7. Explore your narrator's reactions to particular topics, particularly those that arouse emotionally charged responses during the interview.

8. Ask follow-up questions to probe the meaning of events or experiences, but respect your narrator's privacy when she appears reticent to discuss something.

9. Explore how gender shaped your narrator's experience of major historical and cultural events and movements.

10. Through your questions, interest, and actions, validate the assumption that every woman's story matters.

# Appendices

Dr. Ruth Finkelstein promoted women's health

# PRE-INTERVIEW QUESTIONAIRE

_____

1. Name of Narrator: _____
                   First        Middle        Last        Maiden

2. Address: _____
          Street        Apt. no.     City     State   Zip code

   Telephone: (____) _____ (____) _____
             Home             Work/Other

3. Other address, if different from home (e.g. winter or summer residence):

   _____
          Street        Apt. no.     City     State   Zip code

   Telephone: (____) _____

4. Other contact information:  Email address: _____

   Fax: (____) _____ Cell phone: (____) _____ Other: _____

5. Date of birth: _____ Place of birth: _____
                                         Town/City    State/Province    Country

## FAMILY OF ORIGIN:

6. Mother's name: _____
                  First        Middle        Last        Maiden

   Date of birth: _____ Date of death: _____

   Place of birth: _____
                     Town/City       State/Province       Country

   Occupations: _____

7. Father's name: _____
                First         Middle        Last

   Date of birth: _____ Date of death: _____

   Place of birth: _____
                     Town/City       State/Province       Country

   Occupations: _____

8. Name of step-parent, guardian or other: _____

                                                              First                      Middle                   Last

    Date of birth: _____ Date of death: _____

    Place of birth: _____

                            Town/City                        State/Province               Country

    Occupations: _____

9. Siblings: _____

              Name                Date of birth      Date of death      Occupation(s)

    _____

              Name                Date of birth      Date of death      Occupation(s)

    _____

              Name                Date of birth      Date of death      Occupation(s)

10. When and from what city/region/country did your family immigrate to the United States?

    Mother's family: _____ Date: _____

    Father's family: _____ Date: _____

11. If possible, list the places where your parents and grandparents lived:

    Maternal relatives: _____

    Paternal relatives: _____

12. List the main places you have lived, with approximate dates:

    _____

    _____

# RELIGIOUS AFFILIATIONS/IDENTIFICATIONS:

13. While growing up, how did you identify yourself as a Jew?

    _____

14. Did your family belong to a synagogue? If so, list names, denominations, and approximate years of membership.

    _____

    _____

15. How do you currently identify yourself as a Jew?

    _____

16. Do you currently belong to a synagogue? If so, list names, denominations, and approximate years of membership.

_____

_____

17. Were you or your family involved in Jewish communal organizations? If so, list names and years of membership.

_____

_____

# EDUCATIONAL BACKGROUND:

18. Please list all schools attended for your general education:

| School/Location | Course of study | Dates | Degree |
|---|---|---|---|
| School/Location | Course of study | Dates | Degree |
| School/Location | Course of study | Dates | Degree |
| School/Location | Course of study | Dates | Degree |
| School/Location | Course of study | Dates | Degree |

19. Please list all schools attended for your Jewish education:

| School/Location | Course of study | Dates | Degree |
|---|---|---|---|
| School/Location | Course of study | Dates | Degree |
| School/Location | Course of study | Dates | Degree |

# WORK (PAID AND VOLUNTEER):

20. Please list all occupations for which you recieved training: _____

_____

21. Paid employment/jobs held:

| Job title | Employer | Dates |
|---|---|---|
| Job title | Employer | Dates |
| Job title | Employer | Dates |

22. Please list any volunteer work (civic, community, religious, charitable and/or political) that has had any personal significance:

| Organization | Type of work or position | Dates |
|---|---|---|
| Organization | Type of work or position | Dates |
| Organization | Type of work or position | Dates |

23. Hobbies and special interests: _____

# PERSONAL INFORMATION:

24. What best describes your current status (check one):

Married _____ Committed relationship _____ Single _____ Widowed _____ Divorced _____

25. Date of first marriage/committed relationship (if applicable): _____

Husband/Partner's name: _____
First     Middle     Last

Date of birth: _____ If deceased, date of death: _____

Place of birth: _____
First     Middle     Last

Occupation(s): _____

26. Date of second marriage/committed relationship (if applicable): _____

Husband/Partner's name: _____
First     Middle     Last

Date of birth: _____ If deceased, date of death: _____

Place of birth: _____
First     Middle     Last

Occupation(s): _____

27. If you have children, please list:

| Name | Date of birth | Occupation | Place of residence | No. of children |
|---|---|---|---|---|
| Name | Date of birth | Occupation | Place of residence | No. of children |
| Name | Date of birth | Occupation | Place of residence | No. of children |
| Name | Date of birth | Occupation | Place of residence | No. of children |

28. Please describe three significant events or issues in your life that you would like to discuss in an interview. Each of these should reflect different aspects of your life: for example, personal and family, religion, community activities, paid and volunteer work.

1. _____

   _____

   _____

   _____

2. _____

   _____

   _____

   _____

3. _____

   _____

   _____

   _____

29. Please list other historical events (local, regional, national, or international), sociocultural or political changes, or shifts in attitudes that have affected you in a significant way.

   _____

   _____

   _____

   _____

Additional thoughts or comments: _____

   _____

   _____

   _____

Completed by: _____  Date: _____

# PRELIMINARY RELEASE FORM

_____
Organization and Project Title

Name of Narrator: _____     Interview Date(s): _____

Location of Interview: _____

Home Address: _____
                                        Street                                                                    Apt. no.

_____
                 City                                                    State                                          Zip code

Telephone: ( ____ ) _____     ( ____ ) _____
                          Home                                          Work/Other

1. I, the Narrator, acknowledge that I have participated in an interview for the

_____ oral history project and that the
               (Organization and Project Title)

interview was recorded with my full and complete knowledge and consent.

2. I hereby give to _____ the recordings of this interview,
                                            (Organization)

and I grant and assign all rights, title, and interests, including copyright, of whatever kind

from this information and interview to _____ .
                                                                                  (Organization)

3. I understand that my interview may be used by _____ ,
                                                                                                        (Organization)

subject to any restrictions listed below. Such use may include, but is not limited to, publica-

tion in all media (print, graphic, film, and electronic media, including Web sites) currently in

existence or yet to be developed in the future.

4. I understand that, in the future, the _____ intends to
                                                                              (Organization)

donate my interview to local and national repositories for its long-term preservation and use

by scholars, researchers, educators, and the general public.

Signature of Narrator: _____     Date: _____

# FINAL RELEASE FORM

_____
Organization and Project Title

Name of Narrator: _____    Interview Date(s): _____

Location of Interview: _____

Home Address: _____
                            Street                                                     Apt. no.

_____
               City                            State                         Zip code

Telephone: ( _____ ) _____   ( _____ ) _____
                Home                             Work/Other

1. I, the Narrator, acknowledge that I have participated in an interview for the

_____ oral history project and that the
             (Organization and Project Title)

interview was recorded with my full and complete knowledge and consent.

2. I hereby give to _____ the recordings of this interview,
                         (Organization)

and I grant and assign all rights, title, and interests, including copyright, of whatever kind

from this information and interview to _____ .
                                             (Organization)

3. I understand that my interview may be used by _____ ,
                                          (Organization)

subject to any restrictions listed below. Such use may include, but is not limited to, publica-

tion in all media (print, graphic, film, and electronic media, including Web sites) currently in

existence or yet to be developed in the future.

4. Any limitations that I wish to place on the use of the audio recording, transcripts, or pho-

tographs are listed below: _____

_____

Signature of Narrator: _____    Date: _____

# INTERVIEW LOG

_____

Narrator's name: _____ Interview Date: _____
First        Middle       Last

Interviewer's name: _____ Location: _____

Recording I.D. label: _____

Recording format (please check):

**Video**     Type:   ½-inch VHS _____   High-8 _____   Digital _____   Other _____

**Audio**     Type:   Cassette tape ___   Type _____   Length _____

                Sides recordered:   A only ___     A and B ___

                Digital (DAT): ___     Mini-disk: ___     Other: _____

                Speed recorded, if applicable: _____
                                                (normal, LP2, other)

Approximate length of interview: _____
                                  Hours        Minutes

## SUMMARY OF CONTENTS

**Counter Number:**       **Notations:**

Tape/Disk no. _____ of _____ , Side ___

_____       _____

_____       _____

_____       _____

_____       _____

_____       _____

_____       _____

_____       _____

_____       _____

# INTERVIEW LOG PAGE _____

Narrator's name: _____    Date: _____

First          Middle          Last

Oral Historian: _____    Location: _____

Label ID: _____    Approximate Total Length of Interview: _____

**Counter Number:**          **Notations:**

Tape/Disk no. _____ of _____ , Side _____

_____          _____

_____          _____

_____          _____

_____          _____

_____          _____

_____          _____

_____          _____

_____          _____

_____          _____

_____          _____

_____          _____

_____          _____

_____          _____

_____          _____

_____          _____

_____          _____

_____          _____

_____          _____

_____          _____

_____          _____

# PROPER WORD FORM

Organization and Project Title

Name of Narrator: _____     Interview Date(s): _____

Interviewer: _____     Telephone: (_____) _____

Location of Interview: _____

Recording I.D. label: _____

Please list below, in the order recorded, the proper names and other words that a transcriber or researcher might have difficulty spelling or understanding.

1. _____     2. _____

3. _____     4. _____

5. _____     6. _____

7. _____     8. _____

9. _____     10. _____

11. _____     12. _____

13. _____     14. _____

15. _____     16. _____

17. _____     18. _____

19. _____     20. _____

21. _____     22. _____

23. _____     24. _____

Missode Piha, beloved member of Seattle's Sephardic community

# SELECTED BIBLIOGRAPHY
## ON AMERICAN JEWISH WOMEN

ANTLER, JOYCE. *The Journey Home: How Jewish Women Shaped Modern America.* Schocken Books, 1997.

ANTLER, JOYCE, ed. *Talking Back: Images of Jewish Women in American Popular Culture.* University of New England Press, 1998.

ASHTON, DIANNE. *Rebecca Gratz: Women and Judaism in Antebellum America.* Wayne State University Press, 1996.

BAUM, CHARLOTTE, PAULA HYMAN, AND SONYA MICHEL. *The Jewish Woman in America.* Doubleday, 1976.

DINER, HASIA AND BERYL LIEFF BENDERLY. *Her Works Praise Her: A History of Jewish Women in America from Colonial Times to the Present.* Basic Books, 2002.

DINER, HASIA. *Hungering for America: Italian, Irish, and Jewish Foodways in their Age of Migration.* Harvard University Press, 2001.

DINER, HASIA. *Lower East Side Memories: The Jewish Place in America.* Princeton University Press, 2000.

FISHMAN, SYLVIA BARACK. *A Breath of Life: Feminism in the American Jewish Community.* The Free Press, 1993.

GLENN, SUSAN. *Daughters of the Shtetl: Life and Labor in the Immigrant Generation.* Cornell University Press, 1990.

GOLDMAN, KARLA. *Beyond the Synagogue Gallery: Finding a Place for Women in American Judaism.* Harvard University Press, 2000.

GREENBERG, BLU. *On Women and Judaism: A View From Tradition.* Jewish Publication Society, 1994.

HYMAN, PAULA. *Gender and Assimilation in Modern Jewish History: The Roles and Representations of Women.* University of Washington Press, 1995.

HYMAN, PAULA E. AND DEBORAH DASH MOORE, eds. *Jewish Women in America: An Historical Encyclopedia, 2 Vols.* Routledge, 1997.

JOSELIT, JENNA WEISSMAN. *The Wonders of America: Reinventing Jewish Culture, 1880 - 1950.* Hill and Wang, 1996.

MARKOWITZ, RUTH JACKNOW. *My Daughter, the Teacher: Jewish Teachers in the New York City Schools.* Rutgers University Press, 1993.

MOORE, DEBORAH DASH. *To the Golden Cities: Pursuing the American Jewish Dream in Miami and L.A.* The Free Press, 1994.

MORANTZ-SANCHEZ, REGINA. *In Her Own Words: Oral Histories of Women Physicians.* Yale University Press, 1982.

NADELL, PAMELA S., ed. *American Jewish Women's History: A Reader.* New York University Press, 2003.

NADELL, PAMELA S. AND JONATHAN D. SARNA, eds. *Women and American Judaism: Historical Perspectives.* Brandeis University Press/University Press of New England, 2001.

ORENSTEIN, DEBRA. *Lifecycles: Jewish Women on Life Passages and Personal Milestones.* Jewish Lights, 1994.

PRELL, RIV-ELLEN. *Fighting to Become Americans: Jews, Gender and the Anxiety of Assimilation.* Beacon Press, 1999.

ROGOW, FAITH. *"Gone to Another Meeting": The National Council of Jewish Women, 1893-1993.* University of Alabama Press, 1993.

SCHLOFF, LINDA MACK. *"And Prairie Dogs Weren't Kosher": Jewish Women in the Upper Midwest Since 1855.* Minnesota Historical Society Press, 1996.

SCHREIER, BARBARA A. *Becoming American Women: Clothing and the Jewish Immigrant Experience, 1880-1920.* Chicago Historical Society, 1994.

UMANSKY, ELLEN M. AND DIANNE ASHTON, eds. *Four Centuries of Jewish Women's Spirituality: A Sourcebook.* Beacon Press, 1992.

WEINBERG, SYDNEY S. *The World of Our Mothers: The Lives of Jewish Immigrant Women.* University of North Carolina Press, 1988.

WENGER, BETH. *New York Jews and the Great Depression: Uncertain Promise.* Yale University Press, 1996.

## Laurie Schwab Zabin, faculty member at Johns Hopkins

*'I still believe that the strength of Judaism lies a great deal in the woman's role.*

**Sarah Kappelman Harris**

# ORAL HISTORY RESOURCES

## Selected Bibliography on Oral History

BAUM, WILLA K. *Transcribing and Editing Oral History.* Alta Mira Press, 1977.

GLUCK, SHERNA. *"What's So Special about Women?: Women's Oral History,"* in *Oral History: An Interdisciplinary Anthology,* eds. DAVID K. DUNAWAY AND WILLA K. BAUM. Alta Mira Press, 1996.

GLUCK, SHERNA AND DAPHNE PATAI, eds. *Women's Words: The Feminist Practice of Oral History.* Routledge, 1991.

HARTLEY, WILLIAM G. *The Everything Family Tree Book: Finding, Charting, and Preserving Your Family History.* Adams Media Corporation, 1998.

NEUENSCHWANDER, JOHN A. *Oral History and the Law.* Oral History Association, 2002.

ORAL HISTORY ASSOCIATION. *Evaluation Guidelines.* Oral History Association, 2002.

RITCHIE, DONALD A. *Doing Oral History: A Practical Guide (Second Edition).* Oxford University Press, 2003.

SOMMER, BARBARA W. AND MARY KAY QUINLAN. *The Oral History Manual.* Alta Mira Press, 2002.

UNITED STATES HOLOCAUST MEMORIAL MUSEUM. *Oral History Guidelines.* United States Holocaust Memorial Museum, 1998.

## Selected Organizational Resources

American Association for State and Local History
1717 Church Street
Nashville, TN 37203-2991
615-320-3203
www.aaslh.org

Oral History Association
Dickinson College
P.O. Box 1773
Carlisle, PA 17013
717-245-1036
www.dickinson.edu/organizations/oha

H-Oralhist (oral history listserv)
www.h-net.msu.edu/~oralhist/

Jewish Women's Archive
138 Harvard Street
Brookline, MA 02446
617-232-2258
www.jwa.org

DR. JOYCE ANTLER

Joyce Antler is the Samuel Lane Professor of American Jewish History and Culture at Brandeis University, where she teaches in the American Studies Department. She is the author of *The Journey Home: How Jewish Women Shaped Modern America* and the editor of *America and I: Short Stories by American Jewish Women Writers* and *Talking Back: Images of Jewish American Popular Culture*. Antler is a founding member of the Board of Directors of the Jewish Women's Archive and chairs its Academic Advisory Council.

DR. DIANNE ASHTON

Dianne Ashton is Professor of Religion Studies and Director of American Studies at Rowan University. She is the author of *Rebecca Gratz: Women and Judaism in Antebellum America*, *Jewish Life in Pennsylvania*, and, co-editor with Ellen Umansky of *Four Centuries of Jewish Women's Spirituality*.

DR. HASIA DINER

Hasia Diner is the Paul S. and Sylvia Steinberg Professor of American Jewish History at New York University. She is the author of *Lower East Side Memories: The Jewish Place in America*, *Hungering for America: Italian, Irish, and Jewish Foodways in their Age of Migration*, and co-author with Beryl Lieff Benderly of *Her Works Praise Her: A History of Jewish Women in America from Colonial Times to the Present*.

DR. KARLA GOLDMAN

Karla Goldman is Historian in Residence at the Jewish Women's Archive. She is the author of *Beyond the Synagogue Gallery: Finding a Place for Women in American Judaism*. She was the first woman faculty member on the Cincinnati campus of Hebrew Union College – Jewish Institute of Religion where she taught from 1991 to 2000.

DR. JAYNE K. GUBERMAN

Jayne K. Guberman is the Director of Oral History at the Jewish Women's Archive. Since 1998, she has directed Weaving Women's Words, JWA's national initiative to document the life histories of American Jewish women. Guberman co-curated an exhibition entitled Women Whose Lives Span the Century based on JWA's pilot oral history project in Boston and was project director for exhibitions in Baltimore and Seattle inspired by the Weaving Women's Words oral histories.

DR. PAULA E. HYMAN

Paula E. Hyman is Lucy Moses Professor of Modern Jewish History at Yale University. A scholar of modern Jewish history with specialties in French history and women's history, Hyman is the author of *Gender and Assimilation in Modern Jewish History: The Roles and Representation of Women* and co-author of *The Jewish Woman in America*. She is co-editor-in-chief of the two-volume *Jewish Women in America: An Historical Encyclopedia*.

Dr. Jenna Weissman Joselit
Jenna Weissman Joselit teaches American Studies at Princeton University. A columnist for *The Forward*, she is the author of *The Wonders of America: Reinventing Jewish Culture*, and *A Perfect Fit: Clothes, Character and the Promise of America*.

Dr. Regina Morantz-Sanchez
Regina Morantz-Sanchez is Professor of History at the University of Michigan. She is the author of *Conduct Unbecoming a Woman: Medicine on Trial in Turn of the Century Brooklyn*, *Sympathy and Science: Women Physicians in American Medicine*, and *In Her Own Words: Oral Histories of Women Physicians*.

Dr. Pamela S. Nadell
Pamela S. Nadell is Professor of History and Director of the Jewish Studies Program at American University. The author of *Women Who Would Be Rabbis: A History of Women's Ordination, 1889-1985* and *Conservative Judaism in America*, she is the editor of *American Jewish Women's History: A Reader*, and with Jonathan D. Sarna, *Women and American Judaism: Historical Perspectives*.

Dr. Riv Ellen Prell
Riv-Ellen Prell is a professor of American Studies at the University of Minnesota. She is the author of *Prayer and Community: The Havurah in American Judaism* and *Fighting to Become Americans: Jews, Gender, and the Anxiety of Assimilation*.

Joan Roth
For over three decades, Joan Roth has traveled the world to photograph Jewish women in their own environments. Her award-winning photographs have been published and exhibited worldwide. Roth was the photographer for JWA's Weaving Women's Words oral history projects in Baltimore and Seattle. Her photographs appear in the exhibition catalgue, *Weaving Women's Words: Baltimore Stories*, and in the on-line exhibitions on the JWA website, www.jwa.org. Roth has published collections of her photographs titled *The Jews of Ethiopia* and *Jewish Women: A World of Tradition and Change*.

Nicki Newman Tanner
Nicki Newman Tanner is the Chair of the Board of Directors of the Jewish Women's Archive. She is a trustee of several institutions, including the Colonial Williamsburg Foundation, WNYC (New York's public radio stations), Hebrew Union College, and the UJA-Federation of Jewish Philanthropies, where she chairs the Oral History Project. On the Board of Wellesley College for eighteen years, Tanner co-chaired their record-breaking capital campaign.

Dr. Beth Wenger
Beth Wenger is the Katz Family Chair in American Jewish History and Associate Professor of History at the University of Pennsylvania. She is the author of *New York Jews and the Great Depression: Uncertain Promise*; co-editor of *Encounters With the "Holy Land": Place, Past and Future in American Jewish Culture*; and co-editor of *Remembering the Lower East Side: American Jewish Reflections*.

*'I've lived in an extraordinarily wonderful period from 1924 to now. It's over 75 years of extraordinary growth and a narrowing of the world. I think the biggest change is in communication — thank heavens for email!*

Clementine L. Kaufman

Children's book author Molly Cone at her computer

# Help us learn from you!

Please email your comments
and suggestions
to oralhistory@jwa.org.

◇◇◇◇◇◇◇◇◇◇◇◇◇◇◇◇◇◇◇◇◇◇◇◇◇◇◇◇◇◇◇◇◇◇◇◇◇◇◇◇◇◇◇◇◇◇◇◇